To Teresa.

Tom Pilgrim is one of the most successful Spiritualist healers in Britain today. A quiet, unassuming man, he has great power to help people with problems, often those who have tried, and seemingly failed, with the more traditional medical methods.

He is married and lives in Brighton where he sees his patients and also receives around 200 letters a week from people asking his help.

Nadia Fowler is a freelance journalist and has written a number of articles for _Psychic News_.

With Love + Blessings.

Tom Pilgrim.

_25/9/85_

Tom Pilgrim: Autobiography Of A Spiritualist Healer

TOM PILGRIM
WITH NADIA FOWLER

SPHERE BOOKS LIMITED
30-32 Gray's Inn Road, London WC1X 8JL

First published in Great Britain by
Sphere Books Ltd 1982
Copyright © 1982 by Tom Pilgrim and Nadia Fowler

Excerpts from the Hannen Swaffer Home Circle
published by kind permission of Two Worlds
Publications Ltd

TRADE
MARK

Set in Baskerville

Printed and bound in Great Britain by
Cox & Wyman Ltd, Reading

I wish to dedicate this book to my friend the late Maurice Barbanell, Editor of *Psychic News*, for all his encouragement and advice.

My loving thanks go out to my wife, Phyllis, who helped me in my work from the very first day we met.
My thanks also to Geoffrey for his invaluable support in the past and to all those who help with voluntary work in my home in Brighton.

Chapter 1

Childhood

The moment the whistle went I panicked. I was no goalkeeper! Not even in practice games had I ever attempted such a thing. Yet here I was, acting as 'goalie' to our school's football team in the year's most important match.

Only ten minutes before the start it had been discovered that Muggie Moore, our team's goalkeeper, was missing and as no volunteer had come forward to take his place, the sports master had pounced on me:

'Pilgrim, you've got to do it!'

It was no good protesting – before I knew what was happening, I had been propelled onto the pitch. I was twelve years old at the time, enjoyed playing football and was a good inside right. But goalkeeper? Oh no!

'Don't worry,' said Ted Mitchell, who was playing right back, 'the ball won't get anywhere near you. That lot has never scored against us yet.'

All very well, I thought, but there is always a first time! The goal looked enormous. There was no net, only the uprights and the crossbar. How was I to prevent such a small object as a football getting into so large an area? Still, Mitchell seemed to be right. The game was moving back and forth, but never came near my end. I started to relax.

With half time over, I took up my position with more

confidence. I stopped worrying, leant against the upright and watched the game.

Suddenly I became aware of a group of children, much younger than us boys, running on and off the pitch, chasing each other, laughing and quite obviously having a wonderful time. I became enthralled as I watched them. I knew nobody else could see them – they were spirit children; but I had seen such children often, ever since the age of six or seven.

My whole attention was on those kids, when all at once a tremendous scuffling and a voice yelling 'Tom', brought me back to reality. There had been a break-through by the opposing team and I could see that our goal was in imminent danger. 'Ginger', the red-headed boy from the enemy side, had just kicked the ball. It looked like a high shot and I dashed behind the goal to catch it, but to my consternation the ball dipped and went in under the crossbar.

It was a first-class disaster. Watching those spirit kids instead of keeping my attention on the game, lost us the match! No more goals were scored by either team and we were beaten one nil. Our team, the East Hove Secondary School, was top of the League; our opponents, the Loder Road School team, bottom of the League. That we were going to win had been a foregone conclusion.

I was keenly aware of my disgrace, but the worst humili-ation was to come next Monday morning at Assembly. In the presence of about 200 boys our headmaster an-nounced:

'On Saturday we were defeated by bottom of League Loder Road School, and the boy who let us down was Tom Pilgrim! Step forward, Pilgrim, so that all can see you.'

The fatal football match was only one incident in the long drawn-out misery of my schooldays. Although I was a good scholar and did well in most subjects, I was constantly in trouble. Why? Simply because I had been born with a gift that none of my classmates or teachers possessed: the gift of clairvoyance. I saw and heard things that others couldn't.

I should have kept quiet about it, but the spirit children I sometimes saw so clearly in the classroom or on the recreation ground were a source of joy to me which I wanted to share.

Nobody believed me. My classmates laughed and teased me, teachers called me 'liar' or 'foolish dreamer'. I was scolded and punished cruelly, because I would never admit to lying, insisting that I was telling the truth.

My worst tormentor was form-master Dimbleby, generally disliked for his aggressive manner. He never missed an opportunity to ridicule or harass me.

Unfortunately he had eyes as sharp as an eagle's. He could always spot when a boy's attention was elsewhere.

'Pilgrim,' he would thunder, 'what was I saying just now?'

If I couldn't answer he would make me stand up and shower me with abuse.

'Watching your so-called "spirit children" again, were you?' he asked once.

'Yes Sir, sorry Sir,' I mumbled.

'All right then, Pilgrim, go on, tell the class about your invisible friends,' he said with a sarcastic smile.

At this the class burst out laughing. There was great merriment and I was made to feel a complete fool.

Sometimes Dimbleby would come up to my desk on such occasions and hit me – hard. He was a man of violent temper and once hit me with such force that I fell and was knocked unconscious. I was carried down to the washroom and revived with cold water.

I could have reported the incident to the headmaster and can't remember why I didn't. Perhaps I felt it would only make things worse if I complained. So I kept silent.

The only person I confided in was my mother. Herself a medium, she understood the gift she had handed on to me. Her father, John Upfold, a Dorking blacksmith, had also been clairvoyant.

'He isn't fit to be a teacher,' was my mother's comment, when I told her about Mr Dimbleby's behaviour. 'Don't you worry – it's quite natural that you should see spirit children. Like me, you are clairvoyant. When you are a little older I'll explain psychic matters to you more fully. All psychic gifts are gifts from God. Remember that always.'

'Why then won't people believe me, and why do they so get so cross?'

'Because they are ignorant and close their minds to anything they can't understand. They get cross, because somewhere deep down in their hearts they feel that they are wrong. You will encounter such people throughout your life and you will often be ridiculed and reviled. But you will also find help and encouragement. The spirit world will see to that. Never despair, and you will win through.'

Though my mother was very concerned about the treatment I suffered at Mr Dimbleby's hands, she never carried out her intention to see the headmaster. She was simply too busy to get round to it.

We were a very happy, but also a very poor family. My father was a postman. His earnings were meagre, and to contribute her share to the family budget my mother used to go to some of the well-to-do families of Brighton and Hove and cook for them on special occasions. Sometimes she looked after people's houses, going in to clean and air them when the owners were away. She used to take me along and give me a bath in a proper bathroom. I was thrilled when that happened. All those shining taps, and the gleaming white porcelain bath! At home we could only take 'tub-baths'; in those days few houses had bathrooms.

My mother's psychic gifts were of a very high order. If she were living today, she would be recognised as a first class medium; but in her day the 'Witchcraft Act' of 1735 was still in force, and if she had called herself a 'medium' or a 'clairvoyant' she would have run the risk of possible arrest and imprisonment. The Act, which threatened mediums and spiritual healers alike, was repealed in 1951 – too late for my mother.

However, a woman of resource, she found a way of exercising her gifts and even turning them into a small source of income. She invited friends to tea-parties, and every week, quite regularly, about ten or twelve ladies would arrive in the afternoon to 'take tea'.

'When you have finished your tea, turn your cup over,' she would say and then, making her way round the table, proceed to 'read the tea leaves'.

The tea leaves were neither here nor there. She simply used them to disguise her clairvoyance. She was quite a show-woman and made great play of it! Peering earnestly at the pattern of leaves at the bottom of a cup, she would exclaim: 'Oh dear! Oh no! I can't possibly tell you what I see there!' She would then turn the cup upside down again and continue her round.

The lady concerned would plead, 'Minnie, Minnie, please come back,' until my mother returned and 'read her cup'. It was all great fun and if anybody had questioned the 'goings on' at those tea-parties, everybody would have confirmed that it was just a game.

Yet, my mother would frequently give splendid evidence of her clairvoyance on those occasions. Ladies, who had refused to believe something my mother had told them, often came back to confirm that she had been right.

Once, during the First World War, she had told a grief stricken mother that her son, reported 'missing, presumed dead', was alive. Shortly afterwards he returned home – safe and sound.

I was always allowed to be present at the tea-parties. My mother, who had realised that I was psychic when I was still very young, wanted me to observe and learn. I sat watching and listening; silent, intent, and deeply impressed.

At the end of each gathering, I had to go round with a plate to collect the participants' contributions; ostensibly to 'cover expenses for tea and cakes'. This pretence had to be kept up to remain within the law. Some of the ladies used to give very generously. Quite a few were 'regulars', and some visitors would arrive from places outside Brighton and Hove, having heard of my mother's tea-parties from friends.

I used to be very shy about handing the plate around. Quite shocked, in fact, that money was being collected to pay for my mother's clairvoyance. I felt that as a 'gift of God' it should be given free; but my mother only laughed when I told her of my qualms.

'Tom, darling,' she said, 'you'll understand one day. When you're grown up and have to earn your keep, you'll learn that it is not always possible in life to be as generous as you would like to be.'

I didn't realise then how much this extra money was needed to make ends meet.

My father never came to these weekly gatherings; although he himself had no psychic abilities whatsoever, he went along with everything my mother said and did in this respect. He believed in her gifts and knew her to be a genuine medium; but he would have been mortally embarrassed to sit, the only man, among so many ladies.

I can't remember ever seeing a man at these gatherings. Except for me – who did not yet count – it seemed to have been a strictly 'women only' affair.

Despite their eternal money worries, my parents were happy people, devoted to each other.

We had a nice, fairly spacious, home; four rooms in the upper storey of a house we shared with another family. We were friendly with the people downstairs and visited each other frequently.

Once, when I was still a baby, my mother went down to see them, carrying me in her arms. It nearly ended in tragedy: she tripped over her skirt – dresses were worn very long in those days – and fell, just as she was starting to go down to the basement. Miraculously she landed in such a way that, though bruised, she was not seriously hurt. I was held fast in her arms – bawling my head off, but unharmed.

1912 was a sad year for my parents. My mother was expecting another baby and much looking forward to the 'happy event'; but the baby died at birth. It was a girl. My parents were heartbroken; especially my mother who had wished for a daughter. A boy and a girl had been her idea of 'a perfect family'.

I was only two years old at the time and of course knew nothing of my 'lost' litle sister. My parents told me about her later, and I used to think how nice it would have been to have a sister.

One day (I must have been nine or ten), I was sitting in my room doing some homework. Suddenly I heard a child's voice say: 'Hello Tom!'

I looked up, and there, right in front of me, stood a little girl aged about seven. She had fair hair and the loveliest blue eyes I had ever seen. She wore a short, loose dress of exactly the colour of her eyes, and was very pretty.

'My name is Claudia. I'm your sister.'

I just stared at her, speechless. I was used to spirit children visiting me in my room and often chatted and played with them. But, my sister! My very own sister! I was overwhelmed with joy.

'Claudia,' I finally brought out, 'how lovely!' Then, gathering my wits: 'Why didn't you come before? I've been longing to see you!'

'I wasn't allowed to,' she answered.

'Why?'

'Because there's a time for everything in my world. You have to have permission to do things – I'm learning all about your world too, but I think I like mine better.'

We had a long chat that first time; she told me how she was growing up in the spirit world, and that she often visited our mother.

'Mummy can see me too – she's like you, but Daddy can't. I wonder why so few of you can see us.'

From that day on Claudia visited me frequently and sometimes I could catch a glimpse of her on the recreation ground at school. I had asked her not to appear in the classroom during lessons, telling her about my difficulties at school, and she never did.

Some years later, shortly before I left school, she told

me that her special task would be to look after me throughout my earth-life. I know she does, because she comes and talks to me still. She has grown into a beautiful woman and – she explained to me – as you don't grow old in the spirit world, she stays young and beautiful.

This puzzled me. If you die as a child and then grow up in the spirit world, much as you would have done on earth, how come that you suddenly stop and don't grow any older?

'You don't stop suddenly,' my sister elaborated. 'You develop gradually until you reach maturity. It's a spiritual process, really; we do not "age" as you understand it because there's no decay in our world. "Matter" is not of the same, crude substance here as on the physical plane of existence. "Solidified thought" might be an acceptable description of it.

'It's so difficult to explain, Tom. We live in an entirely different world from your three-dimensional one, and though we too have our "natural laws", they differ radically from yours. One of the reasons, for instance, why you have to have "second sight" to see us is that everything here operates on a much higher vibration, to which your physical eyes are not geared. It's the same with sound; physical ears cannot hear us; "second hearing" – you call it clairaudience – is needed to catch the sound vibrations of our speech.'

I've learnt a great deal from such discussions with my sister. Not that I understand it all. I take what she says on trust; but then, of course, I'm lucky – I do 'see' and 'hear' her.

My father had a hobby my mother didn't approve of at all. He was a keen amateur boxer and enjoyed practice bouts with professionals. He would come home with a black eye at times and even be proud of it. He was also quite willing to use his boxing skills outside the ring or the gymnasium.

One summer evening, it was still light, he and my

mother went out for a stroll. Walking round one of the beautiful tree-lined Brighton squares, they heard a woman's voice screaming 'help, help,' a man's voice shouting unintelligible abuse, and sounds of a violent scuffle.

My father tore round the square to the side from where the noise was coming, and saw a man cruelly beating a woman. Outraged, he threw himself on the man, grabbed him by the collar and tore him away from the screaming woman. Then, turning him round with one twist of his arm, so that the man faced him, started to punch him with great relish.

The woman, released from the blows raining down on her, stood still for a moment, bewildered and open mouthed. Then, with a shriek, she launched herself upon my father, belabouring him with her handbag.

'Stop it, stop it,' she yelled. 'How dare you beat my husband! Let go, let go at once!'

Startled, my father loosened his grip on the man and flung him with a violent shove straight into the arms of his wife. Turning on his heels, my father then strode with great dignity across the road to the spot from where my mother had been watching the whole, incredible scene. It had lasted no more than a minute at the most.

'Women,' he snorted when he reached her. 'Did you see that? Screaming for help and then turning on her rescuer.' Bursting out laughing he added, 'Husband and wife! Well, I never! Interfering in married folk's quarrels doesn't seem to pay, does it?'

Another, gentler, hobby of my father's was the theatre; particularly variety shows.

I think I must have been about seven. I still had to go to bed at 6 pm, when one night the door opened and my father came into my room.

'Come on, Tom; get up,' he said.

I blinked at the gaslight – yes, it was still gaslight then – and said: 'It's not morning yet, Dad, is it?'

'No, it's evening, and I'm going to take you to the Hippodrome.'

My excitement knew no bounds. I was dressed in a

9

jiffy. My mother, horrified, tried to stop what she called 'this nonsense', but my father got his way and from then on, every Friday night, he would take me to the Hippodrome. This went on for many years and I saw all the great variety artists of that era. It has left me with a love of variety shows to this day.

I also have vague memories of World War I which date from a period a little before my first visit to the Hippodrome: soldiers and sailors in their uniforms, military bands, posters, and a couple of soldiers billeted on us.

Brighton today is only a pale shadow of the Brighton of my childhood. It was a wonderful place in which to grow up between the two World Wars, and as the years passed I discovered more and more of its joys.

There was so much to do and see. Palace Pier, West Pier, the 'Pierrots' at the end of the West Pier, where Tommy Trinder started; Jack Shephard's Entertainers, where Max Miller became famous, shows on the beach, 'Blind Harry' playing his accordion; the Hippodrome, and the Grand Theatre, where the No. 2 touring companies played and from where I was twice ignobly ejected by the 'bouncer'.

On both occasions someone had shouted a funny or rude remark from the 'gods', where we youngsters always went because it was cheap. I had not been the culprit; but, despite my protests, it was me who was chucked out.

The summers were glorious. I don't know whether it was really so, but there seemed to have been so much more sunshine than we're having today. Maybe one's memory plays tricks; but I remember long, hot summer days during holiday time, when my mother packed sandwiches and bottles of lemonade and turfed me out of the house at 8 o'clock in the morning. Off I would go with my mates, down to the sea.

When the tide was out, we would search for shells, crabs, or any other treasures the waves left stranded on the wet sand. We would run for miles along the beach, and when the tide was in we would swim and lark about in the water for hours.

Looking back to those far off childhood days, I find my view that life always offers compensations confirmed: I may have had a miserable time at school, but it was amply compensated by the many joys I experienced outside the classroom.

Chapter 2

1924-1942

Everything, good or bad, comes to an end, and one fine day I found myself tearing down the street towards home singing 'no more school, no more school,' at the top of my voice.

I think I must have been the happiest boy in Brighton that day.

My new-found freedom did not last long, however, for times were hard and it was necessary for me to find work and contribute something to the family income.

Jobs weren't that easy to find in 1924; certainly not for a fourteen-year-old school-leaver, and when I was offered a job at a leather workshop where they made and sold suitcases, handbags, attaché cases and the like, I accepted it gratefully.

I stayed four years in that job. The general idea had been that I should learn the trade and stay in it for good; but I soon began to feel that this was not what I wanted to do in life.

Not that I knew what I wanted! Anyway, I got increasingly bored and restless and shortly after my eighteenth birthday I went to the labour exchange to look for a different job.

'I have just one vacancy that might suit you,' said the chap who interviewed me. 'Would photography interest you?'

'Oh yes,' I answered, 'I'd like that.'

The idea appealed very much to me and off I went to present myself at Taylor's photographic company in West Street, Brighton; to my great joy I was taken on.

After a year's training, learning the technical side of the photographic trade: developing, printing, enlarging and retouching, I joined the regular staff.

The work was interesting and varied. I was delighted with my new job.

Years later I realised that I must have been guided to take that particular job; for a train of events started there that was to lead me, after many years of gathering experience, and through much pain and heartbreak, to the point where my life's true vocation was to become clear to me.

At the time, however, there wasn't a cloud in the sky. Life spread before me with all its promise of happiness and success, and in my youthful enthusiasm I accepted all it had to offer with an untroubled heart.

I was still aware of that 'other world' which had been so much part of my childhood; but I had learnt my lesson! I told nobody of my psychic faculties. Only at home, with my parents, did I discuss psychic matters.

Spirit children still showed themselves, even at work, but I never let on.

What pleased me very much was that now my grandfather on my mother's side, John Upfold, known as the 'psychic blacksmith' during his earth-life, came to visit me at times. He often gave me good advice – not that I always followed it.

There were others, too, that came. My father's parents, for instance; but I was going through a period where 'earthly matters' were predominant in my mind and – except for John Upfold's and my sister's appearances – I tended to look at these other-worldly intrusions as an unwelcome distraction.

For one thing, I had fallen in love. When my attention was not on my work, it was wholly upon 'her'.

She was a fellow employee at Taylor's; an enchanting,

13

dark-haired little girl, about my own height, with soft brown eyes and quiet, gentle ways. Her name was Florence.

'Can I help you, Mr Man?' she had enquired one day when she saw me going to the dark room with a great pile of films to be developed.

For some reason I cannot recall, I was always 'Mr Man' to her – until I became 'her' Tom!

I accepted her help gratefully, because there was always a great deal of developing and printing to be done. Gradually her 'helping Mr Man' became an established procedure.

She was shy and rather reserved and it took me a long time before I plucked up courage to ask her to come out with me. I was still only eighteen when we first met and a little on the shy side myself.

By and by, however, shyness melted away and before either of us realised what was happening, we had fallen in love with each other.

Like any other young couple we would go for long walks together, swim in the sea during the summer months and go to the theatre or the cinema at night. On special occasions, during holidays, we would go on day trips to London to 'see the sights', returning to Brighton tired and footsore from walking the London pavements – but blissfully happy.

One thing I was never allowed to forget, though, was the plight of the poor. I remembered my parents' struggle for existence when I was still a child and I resolved to help wherever and whenever I could.

In those days Brighton's poor had to appear before the 'Board of Guardians' and go through the dreaded 'means test' if they wanted assistance; even for small sums like five shillings or seven shillings and sixpence for a pair of shoes, or coal, or whatever, they had to go through this degrading procedure.

Shortly after I had become a fully fledged member of Taylor's staff, I started to accompany applicants to the 'Board of Guardians' to give them moral support and speak up for them if possible.

I was appalled by the treatment meted out to those people. The officials questioning them were heartless and rude. Applicants would tremble before them and often burst into tears.

More than once I lost my temper and shouted at the officials. They threatened to bar me from the proceedings, but I stood my ground and, I think, earned their grudging respect, for they never did throw me out.

I am sure it was spirit guidance that led me to undertake this voluntary job in the service of others – just to prevent me from becoming too materialistic.

The first time I took Florence home to meet my parents, my father was delighted with her. She was so pretty and had such pleasant manners.

My mother said little, which disappointed me, but I knew that she never made snap decisions about people and liked to keep her first impressions to herself until she felt sure about them. So I didn't worry.

Subsequent visits always went off pleasantly enough, except that I sometimes caught my mother gazing at Florence with a questing, probing look in her eyes. This made me uneasy. I knew that look. It meant that she was using her clairvoyant faculty and I wondered what she 'saw'.

One evening, when I returned after taking Florence home, I found my mother waiting for me in the sitting room. My father had gone up to bed.

'Come and talk to me, Tom,' she said, patting the seat beside her on the settee.

I sat down apprehensively. I knew she wanted to talk about Florence.

Taking my hand in hers she said: 'Tom, I like your girl. Florence is a nice kid, but she is very young, and so are you. Go carefully. She is your first love and "first love" is not always "the" love! In short, don't get too attached to Florence. It is not something that will last.'

At that time Florence had been 'my girl' for nearly two years. I was now twenty, Florence nineteen, and there was a tacit understanding between us that we would get married one day, though no firm plans had yet been made.

My mother's gentle warning disturbed me, but I pushed the thought aside and consoled myself with the fact that for the present no final decisions were expected of me.

When I was twenty-one a great opportunity came my way. With the help of a friend much older than me, who treated me almost like a son, I was able to start my own business.

Herbert Jones was a jewel of a man. He gave me not only his expert advice, but also the necessary capital to buy the equipment I needed.

'You can pay me back by and by,' he said, brushing aside my doubts. He had complete confidence in my ability to make a success of the venture.

So I became the proud owner of 'The Brunswick Photo Service'. It did well from the start; orders coming mainly from chemists who sent in roll-films for developing.

In the summer, when visitors thronged the Brighton and Hove beaches, taking their holiday shots, business was brisk. The winter months were more difficult. With the end of September the summer season, and with it the orders from chemist shops, stopped. I had to think of something to keep me going through the winter.

By now I had not only mastered the technical side of my trade, but also the art of taking good pictures. This gave me an idea: why not go into people's houses and take photos of them in their own surroundings?

I invented a slogan: 'Photos by your Fireside' and was overwhelmed by the response. In answer to my advertising this service I was inundated by requests to come and take 'Fireside Photos'.

It was not only a huge success, I also thoroughly enjoyed the work. I used to group a family round a blazing fire, with parents, sometimes also grandparents, sitting or standing near the fireside, and the children sitting on the hearthrug in front of it.

My debts to Herbert Jones were soon paid off and by

the time I was twenty-two I was well established.

The relationship between Florence and me had deep-
ened. My mother, acutely aware of this, warned me
several times not to tie myself down; but I was too deeply
in love to take her words to heart. Florence had become as
precious to me as life itself.

In 1932 we decided to get married. When I told my
mother she said: 'Tom, don't go through with this
marriage; it'll go wrong if you do, and in the end she will
let you down. It's not that Florence is a bad girl or
anything like that; but she is not "yours", you are not
meant for each other.'

Of course, I didn't listen. I had only to look at
Florence, to see her love for me shining from her eyes,
and any doubts I may have had would vanish. In this
case, surely, my mother was wrong!

It seemed that I was right, for the years that followed
were years of great happiness. The only thing that tended
to upset me was Florence's unreasoning jealousy; but,
even if her possessiveness was irksome at times – was it
not also proof of her love?

My mother never again mentioned her misgivings.
Once Florence and I were married she accepted her as a
daughter-in-law with all the loving kindness that was
her nature.

If trouble lay in the future, it cast no shadow into the
present.

My business thrived, and my 'photographer's career'
expanded from fireside photos to a whole range of photographic ventures. With a great deal of youthful nerve I
would, for instance, gate-crash into garden parties and
dances, wearing a 'Press Photographer' badge a friend
had given me, and take pictures of the guests; rushing the
proofs through before the end of the event, whereupon I
would return and take orders.

Or I would walk along the beaches, taking photos of
holiday makers enjoying their sea-side activities; on
Sundays I would go to the Palace Pier and, having made

friends with the Pier Master, sit in his office to await the arrival of celebrities; then, with me in tow, the Pier Master would greet some famous guest, and I would take pictures.

I met many of the stage and film stars that way and remember being deeply impressed by Gracie Fields' vivacious personality.

One day, walking along Brighton promenade, I came upon an elephant. Yes, an elephant! He and his keeper were standing quietly at the edge of the promenade, near the rails, gazing out to sea.

What a lovely subject for a photographer! But I had a better idea than just to take a shot of them as they stood there. I went up to the keeper and asked him if he would like to earn ten shillings – a lot of money then.

'Yes,' he answered, he'd like that very much; what did he have to do for it?

'Could you take the elephant across the "Belisha" crossing to the other side? I'd like to take a shot of him when he's on the crossing.'

'Sure, no problem there, gov'nor.'

I went into the road, halted the traffic, and at a sign from me the keeper sent the elephant across, following a few paces behind him.

I got a magnificent picture, showing the elephant in the middle of the crossing, with all the cars waiting on either side and the Brighton Aquarium in the background. As the keeper was not in the pictures, it looked as if the elephant was crossing by himself.

When I rang the *Daily Mirror* in London, and asked if the picture would interest them, they asked me to send it by rail and they would collect it at Victoria Station.

I looked through the *Daily Mirror* every morning and after a week, when I'd almost given up seeing it published, there was my photo, right across the centre page, with the heading: *'Be like Jumbo, play it safe.'*

This venture got me four guineas – a royal sum in those good old days!

*

If the emphasis was mainly on material things during that particular period of my life, it didn't mean that I'd lost interest in spiritual matters.

The concepts of 'free will' and 'destiny' or 'fate' exercised my mind a great deal at that time – were they not irreconcilable? My marriage, for instance, against which my mother had warned me so consistently and which nevertheless had turned out such a success: was it 'fate' or had I simply exercised my 'free will'?

My mother had once explained to me that 'free will' was one of the most important gifts to man and no one, not even the best intentioned spirit helper, was allowed to interfere with it, for only by the right exercise of our free will could we spiritually grow and develop.

'We have limited free will within the pattern of our lives,' she said, 'but certain events are predestined and inevitable. They are part of our "destiny" or "Karma" as Eastern peoples would call it.'

My mother's teachings were often confirmed by spirit entities like her father, or my sister; though the latter would point out that she herself was still learning and that there was much she couldn't understand yet, let alone explain.

Spirit help and advice was sometimes given to me in quite mundane matters; when I photographed the 'Queen Mary' on her maiden voyage in 1936, for instance.

The Brighton manager of the pharmaceutical department of the Co-op had asked me to take a picture of the event, for display in his shop.

It proved to be quite a hazardous undertaking. When I had got myself to Southampton harbour I found about fifty steamers milling around, each captain jockeying for position; everybody trying to get as near as possible to the 'Queen Mary'.

The steamer I was on got pretty close to its target and tilted alarmingly as all its passengers rushed to one side of the deck to get a good view. I took one look at that cluster of people and dashed below deck.

'Hey you! You want to commit suicide?' shouted a

member of the crew as I squeezed through a porthole and sat on its ledge.

One of the ropes used for tying up the steamer on landing was lying nearby and I quickly grabbed it and wound it round my left arm; then, just as the 'Queen Mary' came at us, I dropped into the Solent up to my knees, and held by the rope, took my picture.

Pleased as punch I reappeared on deck, soaked to the skin, my suit ruined.

The picture came out a treat! It was so clear, you could see the people on deck. I made a large copy of it, split into three sections, to fit all along the wall at the Co-op shop. The manager was delighted and later ordered postcard size copies. They sold by the dozen. I also made a slide from the negative and all the Brighton cinemas showed it.

Surely I had been given 'help' in that venture! I had acted on a strong impulse when I got myself below deck and through the porthole. Once in position, I had only seconds to take the picture; a fraction of a second later the chance would have been lost.

On 13 June, 1938, my son Alan was born. Florence and I were overjoyed. We had both wanted our first born to be a boy.

Life seemed perfect – but not for long. It was impossible to ignore the happenings in the world outside our small family circle. As news of Hitler's aggressive policies became more and more alarming, I was gripped by uneasy forebodings. I received no spirit warnings or assurances that the crisis would pass, nor did my mother. It was as if the spirit world, too, was holding its breath, waiting for the storm to break.

When war finally did break out in September 1939 our little private world began to change rapidly.

The materials I needed for my photographer's trade first became scarce, then unobtainable, and I had to give up my business.

Once again I was lucky: the Co-op, who was my biggest customer and whose photographic department had closed down for the same reasons, asked me to join them as storekeeper in their pharmaceutical department.

I was in fact doubly lucky; working in the Co-op's pharmaceutical section I was now in a 'reserved occupation' and my call-up was deferred.

In 1940 disaster struck. Enemy air-raids had started in earnest. One night bombs hit the Odeon Cinema in Brighton, causing many casualties and in the same raid the house where my parents lived was destroyed and my father killed. My mother was injured and taken to hospital. She was, however, not seriously hurt and left hospital after a week.

My father's death was a terrible blow; especially to my mother and it was only her firm belief in our continued existence after physical death that kept her going.

It had always been a disappointment to me that Florence showed no interest in psychic matters. She never ridiculed my mother's or my own clairvoyant faculties, but she couldn't bring herself to really 'believe' in them.

She had been very fond of my father and had genuinely grieved over his passing. So when he 'showed' himself, which he did not long after his death, I told her about it; but I couldn't convince her of the reality of what I 'saw' and 'heard'.

My mother now lived with us. We had ample space and it worked out well. I was very happy to have her around. She was a great help to Florence in her household duties and little Alan was delighted that Granny, whom he loved dearly, was now part of our household.

Still in 1940 and not long after my father had been killed, I lived through an experience that shook me to the core.

Every Sunday I used to take Alan on an 'outing'; the two of us, father and son, would go off on our own. Usually I took him on a short train journey – he loved that – but one Sunday, just for a change, I took him for a walk on the Downs. He was only a little over two years old at the time.

As we were walking along I heard the sound of aircraft; far away at first, but rapidly coming nearer. When they were almost overhead, I could see they were enemy aircraft, flying in formation.

I had just pointed them out to Alan when one plane broke formation, wheeled round, and came straight at us, guns blazing. Quick as lightning I threw the boy into some thick bushes and dived after him. All around us machine gun bullets hit the ground, but we remained unharmed. There were other people on the Downs that day and we heard later that there had been casualties.

As I crawled from the protecting bush, a screaming Alan in my arms, I saw the plane wheeling back into formation. Had the pilot gone in for a bit of private 'fun' – machine gunning defenceless civilians walking on the Downs? There was no way of knowing. None of the other planes did likewise. They swarmed overhead in orderly formation and soon disappeared on the horizon; as we heard later, to drop their bombs on the army and air force camps of Hassocks and Burgess Hill.

Our guns had opened up and there was a hell of a din, in the middle of which an excited Home-Guard soldier came running towards us, shouting if I'd seen any parachutists coming down!

Well, no, I hadn't, but I was badly shaken. The whole incident had lasted but a couple of minutes, and all I had been conscious of was a 'presence' – I cannot describe it in any other way, for I 'saw' nothing – urging me into instant action, almost before I realised the danger.

Poor little Alan! He'd landed in a bramble bush and was covered with scratches. His mother was none too pleased with me when we reached home ...

I was called up into the RAF in 1941 and sent to a camp near Blackpool to train as a storekeeper.

I objected strongly. My real profession was that of a photographer and I wanted to join as such; but it was no good. They had decided on 'storekeeper' for me and that's what I had to be.

After our 'passing-out parade' had been held I went into Blackpool to see Gypsy Rose Lee – then a famous clairvoyant.

'You'll never be sent overseas, dear,' she said.

Well, she must have been on the wrong beam, because that same night we had to 'fall in', and standing to attention on the football field were told that we were being sent overseas!

We were not told where we were going but next morning we were issued with tropical kit. Our guess that we were being sent to the Far East later proved right.

Then came the line-up for vaccination. When my turn came I said: 'I object to vaccination.'

The flight sergeant, who had never before heard an airman make such an outrageous statement, first turned red, then purple in the face and bawled: 'Fall out, Pilgrim!'

I was sent to see the medical officer, and to him I told my story.

My parents didn't believe in vaccination and I had never been vaccinated or inoculated against anything. My mother had given me a booklet: *The Case against Vaccination*, and after reading it I had wholeheartedly agreed with her opinion that it was wrong to poison the bloodstream with serums.

There was no difficulty at school. Vaccination was not compulsory; but when war broke out I knew that sooner or later I would be faced with the vaccination problem. I went to my solicitor to ask his advice, and he sent me to a Justice of the Peace, who gave me a certificate, stating my legitimate objection to vaccination.

It was quite a hilarious procedure. After I had stated my case the Justice of Peace, a kindly old man, said: 'Right, my son; just stand up and say something.'

'What shall I say?'

'Oh, anything you like.'

So I got up from my chair and said:

'I object to vaccination because ...' and didn't get any farther. The old man held up his hand:

'That'll do,' he said and handed me a signed certificate,

23

stating that on valid reasons I was allowed to refuse vaccination.

This certificate I now handed to the MO.

To my great relief he was not only sympathetic, but most interested in what I had to say, and when I showed him the booklet outlining the whole case against vaccination, he asked if he could borrow it.

I was excused vaccination and innoculation on this and many other occasions – until I faced the same problem when I arrived overseas.

'Are you married, have you any dependants?' asked the MO.

'Yes, Sir.'

'Well, Pilgrim, in that case, if you fall sick we shall blame it on your having refused vaccination, and your dependants will get no compensation in case of your invalidity or death.'

So they got me in the end, and I had to submit to vaccination against my deeply held conviction that it was wrong. I still feel aggrieved about it.

The last time I saw Florence before I was sent overseas was when she came to visit me at Bournemouth, where I had been stationed for a month before being sent to the Blackpool camp; once in Blackpool I was more or less cut off. We were given no home leave before sailing, because no one was to know when or where we were going.

Florence came with little Alan, and was I glad to see them! I had no idea at that time if and when I might be sent overseas, but I had a strong presentiment that I'd soon be separated from my family.

My wife must have felt the same, for when the parting came she clung to me sobbing.

'Don't let them send you away, Tom! Whatever would I do without you?'

My heart felt heavy as I tried to comfort her; what could I say to reassure her? It was most probable that I would be sent abroad.

I told her that thousands of families all over Britain were facing the same problem. I asked her to be brave and

24

confident – even if I were sent away. God would surely guide me safely back to her; but when I took my little son into my arms to kiss him goodbye, there were tears in my eyes too.

Chapter 3

War

We embarked at the George V Docks, Clydeside, Scotland, for South Africa, first destination on our long trip to the Far East.

It was a perilous voyage. We sailed in a long convoy of troopships, flanked by destroyers, the famous warship *Ark Royal* – later sunk in enemy action – bringing up the rear.

Convoys were in constant danger of attacks from above or below. When enemy aircraft or German submarines were spotted pandemonium broke out: the destroyers would be all over the place, giving the 'scatter' signal on their hooters; this meant an 'alert' was on and the convoy had to break up instantly. The ships would scatter far and wide and it seemed a miracle to me that our convoy, or what was left of it, managed to reform after such occasions.

One such alert spread over two days. At times the din was indescribable: destroyers hooting, anti-aircraft guns blazing and the *Ark Royal* flinging out depth charges. Much later we were told the *Ark Royal* had sunk two enemy submarines during that encounter.

We had a detachment of Commandos on our ship – the roughest lot of guys you ever saw. Some were toughies released from prison on volunteering to join the Commandos. None of the other troops on board would go anywhere near their quarters, because of the rough games and pranks they liked to play.

One of their favourite 'jokes' was to get hold of an unfortunate RAF or army lad and put him before a 'Kangaroo Court' on some charge. A mock trial would be held, complete with prosecutor, defence lawyer and judge and jury; if the 'defendant' was found guilty – and he always was – he was stripped naked and his clothes and equipment scattered all over the ship.

It may be imagined what the sergeant major of the 'guilty' man's unit had to say to such goings on! It was not the Commandos he would take to task. Not even the toughest of sergeant majors would have dared to do that. No, it was 'his' soldier or airman who would get it in the neck for being so stupid and letting himself be trapped by the Commandos. I was lucky; they never harmed me. I could even go to their quarters without getting into trouble.

Many of my RAF pals, and some of the army lads on board too, were very interested in Spiritualism. We used to have debates on the subject.

Was it the war, the danger, the proximity of death that made men's minds more receptive? I don't know, but I remember being surprised at finding so few scoffers.

I was lying out on deck one night as I often did; it was far too hot and stuffy down below. We had already crossed the equator and above me stretched the velvety night sky of the southern hemisphere, strewn with myriads of stars.

Sleep would not come; I looked up at the incredibly bright stars, conscious of how far from home I was.

I had been able to post a letter to Florence before we embarked; just telling her and my mother that we were on our way to an 'unknown destination' and giving them my RAF posting number, to which they could address their letters.

How would Florence cope without me? She was still so young, so vulnerable. Fear gripped me: would I ever return home? Ever see my little boy again? What if I were killed?

I closed my eyes, shutting out the sight of those alien

27

stars – and at that precise moment I heard a voice say very clearly: 'Do not be afraid. You will be taken care of, and if you never kill another human being you will come back home safely.'

I have no idea whose voice it was that gave me comfort and reassurance that night. When I opened my eyes again I found myself as alone as before in my corner on deck; but I never forgot the voice nor its message and throughout the war I never killed anyone.

Our arrival at Durban was truly memorable. As we neared the harbour, lined up on deck ready to disembark, a woman's voice came across to us as clear as a bell with a choice selection of all the songs the troops loved, ending with 'There'll always be an England' as we tied up at the moorings.

It was the then famous South African opera singer Pera Siedle, known to American troops as 'Kate Smith' or 'Ma', to the Poles in the British services as the 'South African Nightingale' and to the British as the 'Lady in White', because she always appeared at the quayside dressed in white.

Her 'wharfside-work', as she called it, had started in April 1940, when she was saying farewell to a young Irish seaman.

'Please sing something Irish,' he had yelled across the water as his ship pulled out, and through her cupped hands she had answered with 'When Irish eyes are smiling'.

From then to the end of the war she sang to every troopship entering or leaving Durban harbour.

We were posted to Clairwood transit camp, about a mile and a half out of Durban, before being sent on the next lap of our journey.

It was a fantastic time! The 'Boys in Blue', as we were called, were welcome everywhere. Invitations for us to visit Durban families poured into the camp. I proved to be particularly lucky when I was chosen to be the guest of Tom Ramsay, editor of the *Rand Daily Mail*. He and his wife treated me as one of the family; not only did I spend countless happy hours at their beautiful home, they also

28

introduced me to many interesting people in Durban and took me to some fabulous parties. In fact, quite a longstanding friendship developed between us and two years later Tom Ramsay was to play a big part in cutting military red tape and helping me to get back home.

Our Durban interlude passed all too quickly and one day we were back on another troopship, in another convoy, heading for Burma. It was an uneventful voyage.

At our Chittagong base the fleshpots of Durban were soon forgotten, for the Burma war campaign had its particular horrors, as we soon found out.

Yet, we were lucky; the RAF bases lay well behind the lines and we never had to bear the brunt of the fighting, nor the hardships the lads in the infantry had to face.

Our planes used to fly off on bombing raids at half hourly intervals, ranging as far as Rangoon. I belonged to a repair and salvage unit, sent out to locate missing planes and their pilots. We usually found the crashed planes, the decapitated bodies of crews lying nearby, sometimes horribly mutilated.

I once came upon the hardly recognisable remains of a pilot I had known well. The horror of the sight made my stomach heave. I turned aside and vomited. After that I tried not to look too closely at the gruesome finds we made in the course of our duties.

Not that our side had a completely clean sheet. Cruelty begets cruelty and compassion dies where hatred rules.

I remember the Japanese sniper we once caught hiding in the bush not far from our camp. We were bringing him in when we happened to meet a small detachment of Scottish soldiers.

'What are ye going to do with that Jap?' one tall lad asked.

'We're taking him to our CO,' he was told.

'Oh no, ye don't! We take no prisoners,' was the reply, and raising his rifle he split the Jap's skull with one mighty blow of the butt.

A gruesome incident, which I shall never forget.

Our repair and salvage sorties brought us near the fighting lines at times and the front line boys could be pretty scathing about 'Churchill's Blue Orchids', as they used to call the RAF. No wonder! Some of them standing up to their waists in machinegun pits, they were constantly in the thick of it whilst we returned to the safety of our base behind the lines.

Shortly after the incident with the unfortunate Jap sniper I was posted to Asansol in Bengal.

Again I was attached to a repair and salvage unit and my duties remained the same.

I liked Asansol. Our Commanding Officer, Flight Lieutenant Bird, was a wonderful man with a great sense of humour. His men not only respected him as a very competent Commander, they loved and trusted him and consequently we were a happy bunch of chaps.

To relieve the monotony of camp life he had arranged weekly 'get-togethers'; a relaxed hour or so of an evening, when we would sit around smoking our cigarettes, the CO puffing at his pipe and everybody airing his views. You were allowed to let off steam and grumble at anything you liked; the camp's Padre too would join in. You could criticise the camp, the work, the war effort, even Churchill or the Royal family. Nothing was barred. We called these meetings 'grouse nights' and thoroughly enjoyed them.

The Japs used to fly over on bombing raids. They did the same at Chittagong, but their efforts were never very successful, their bombs usually dropping miles off target.

There were occasions when larger attacks by air and on the ground were expected and then everybody in the camp was ordered to carry a rifle and be on the alert.

On one such raid the enemy came pretty close. Planes dropped anti-personnel bombs and Japanese military units were trying to advance on our base. Our guns opened up on the planes and managed to drive them off before too much damage had been done and on the ground the Japs had to tangle with our troops and not many got through. Those who did were quickly disposed of.

I, mindful of the warning I had received on the voyage to Durban, shot in the air!

It was during the Asansol period that my mail suddenly stopped. At first I was not particularly worried, because we were known as the 'forgotten army' out there and mail could get badly held up. Supplies, if they came at all, always came late and we were often desperately short of spare parts for the repair of our planes. Pilots used to fly off in Blenheim bombers patched up with wire.

But as weeks lengthened into months and still no letter came from home I grew anxious. My pals were receiving their mail, so there was no postal hold up. Every time mail arrived it was the same answer:

'Sorry, Tom, no, there's nothing for you.'

My imagination began working overtime: my home had been hit in an air-raid; Florence and Alan had been killed; my mother was dead, too; or perhaps they were all lying in hospital, grievously injured, mother and Florence unable to write? Thus ran my thoughts. Over and over again I tried to figure out what may have happened. Why was I not hearing from them? Round and round in a circle. The memory of Florence clinging to me at our parting, sobbing 'don't leave me, whatever should I do without you?' haunted me day and night.

After three months came the breakdown. I couldn't concentrate on my work, couldn't sleep, couldn't eat. Worst of all, I received no help from the spirit world. Not a word came across to me; not even from my sister. I seemed cut off from all that was dear to me in this world and the next.

Finally, in despair, I went to our CO.

'I'm finished, Sir,' I said. 'I won't work any more, you can take me off all my duties. I'm leaving the RAF and I'm leaving *now*.'

Flight Lieutenant Bird, surely one of the kindest, most

understanding COs ever to grace the RAF, gave me a long, searching look.

'At ease, Pilgrim,' he said. I had been standing stiffly to attention.

'Come on, man, sit down and tell me all about it.'

I sat myself on the chair facing his makeshift desk and repeated:

'I've had it, Sir, I'm sorry, but I'm no longer in the RAF.' I saw his eyebrows go up and the corners of his mouth twitch; then he broke out laughing:

'Good God, Pilgrim! What do you mean by "I'm no longer in the RAF?" You *are* in the RAF. Nobody can walk out just like that!' Then, in a kindly tone of voice: 'I've noticed your being out of sorts – what's happened? Come on, tell me, you know I'll do all I can to help.'

His kindness had me close to tears, but I pulled myself together and told him about my anxieties; how worry over my lack of news from home was tormenting me; that I was sure something dreadful had happened to my family.

'I think you should have a word with our Padre, Pilgrim. He'll be able to help you better than I can in this case.'

The Padre was the last person I wanted to see, but there was nothing I could do except follow the Commander out of his tent. We found the Padre standing in front of the small hut that served as 'chapel', and after a few explanatory words the CO left us.

I had to tell my story all over again and did so with difficulty. I must have been almost incoherent, but the Padre seemed to get the gist of it and at the end of my rambling account he suggested I should go into the chapel with him for a quiet prayer.

At this I lost my patience.

'Prayer won't help,' I shouted, and anyway, I'd lost my faith and wasn't going into any chapel.

That was too much for the good Padre who happened to be a giant of a man. He just grabbed me and tried to push me into the chapel. I broke loose, whereupon he grabbed me again, pushed me in the direction of the chapel; I tore myself free, he grabbed me – and this tug-of-war went on until my strength gave out and he got me inside.

'Come on now, calm yourself, kneel down with me and we'll pray together.'

By this time I was completely exhausted; my resistance broken, I knelt down and gradually felt myself returning to some semblance of sanity.

We sat down after the Padre had finished his prayer: 'Feeling better now?' he asked.

I said I did and apologised for my disgraceful behaviour.

'You should have come to me straight away, son; I have more strings to pull than the CO – I can find out about your family. I'll send a signal and by tomorrow we'll have the answer.'

I couldn't believe it. How could the Padre send a signal and get an answer back to this godforlorn place the next day?

He did, though! In the late afternoon I saw the Padre coming towards the spot where we were playing a very primitive game of cricket; he was waving a piece of paper.

It was a telegram: 'Wife and child all right will write Brighton Police' it read.

I almost cried for joy. Thank God! They were well and safe. Not long afterwards the promised letter from Florence arrived and life was worth living again.

My mother wrote too. She had been ill with some infection, but was now fully recovered. Florence had had her hands full, what with my mother's illness, looking after Alan, and doing some voluntary war work. She was sorry about the long letter-writing pause and promised to write regularly.

Trouble seldom comes singly and hardly had my domestic problems been solved, when my health broke down.

For some time I had suffered from occasional earache. Nothing serious, I had thought; but now, suddenly, I got the most excruciating pains. On examination it was discovered that my eardrums had been perforated. Gunfire, bombs exploding, the whole hideous din of war had taken its toll.

I was taken to the sick bay, a glorified marquee, where I stayed for nearly four weeks. The pain I suffered was so intense at times that I went berserk and three blokes had to sit on me to keep me down. Painkilling drugs were almost unobtainable, they were in such short supply.

Eventually I was sent to the military hospital at Calcutta and slowly recovered. That is my ears mended, but there was something wrong with my feet too – seriously wrong. Walking was agony, my feet hurt so much.

Some would say that what happened next was coincidence; but to me it proved that the voice that had said '. . . you will be taken care of', when I was shaken by fear on the voyage out from Britain, was keeping its promise: I was being guided and guarded. No one will convince me that it was 'coincidence' that just at that time a famous Harley Street orthopaedic surgeon was visiting the Calcutta military hospital.

After advising me of the risks I would take as a 'medical guinea pig', he performed an operation on my feet that had never been attempted before. It was the only hope of ever getting my feet back to normal again.

The operation was a complete success, and to the joy of the surgeon, the nurses and last but not least to myself, I was up after six weeks in bed and learning to walk normally again.

There followed another six weeks at a military convalescence home 6,000 feet high in the mountains. I had a wonderful time there. In that clear mountain air even the 'prickly heat' from which we all suffered disappeared.

One thing I remember vividly was playing football against members of a Ghurka regiment. They played barefoot! And we could never beat them.

At my final medical the MO said: 'How would you like to walk along Brighton seafront again?'

34

'I'd like that very much, Sir,' I answered, not knowing what he was getting at.

He just grinned at me, shuffled all my medical papers and reports together, rolled them up and blew through them as if through a trumpet.

'Bugle call to freedom, Pilgrim! Off you go.'

I was being posted home! I could hardly believe my luck, but in no time I was cleared from the station and on my way back to Durban. From there a Red Cross train took me to Petermartsburgh, where I landed in another hospital.

After two weeks I was given a second medical; this time by South African doctors, who, to my dismay, pronounced me fit to stay on duty in South Africa until the end of the war.

I was posted to Johannesburg, to work as a clerk at a military hospital.

Shattered by this setback – I'd already seen myself on Brighton's Promenade – I 'phoned the Ramsays in Durban.

'Tom!' Mrs Ramsay's voice was full of delighted surprise, and when I told her that I'd been given a week's leave she said: 'Wonderful! We'll pick you up and you'll stay with us.'

Back in Johannesburg I had the good fortune to meet Carrie Rothkugel, a highly influential lady. She used to act as hostess for General Smuts at official occasions; General Smuts' wife being a very simple Dutch woman who lacked the 'social graces' expected of the 'first lady of the land'.

Carrie Rothkugel was also known as the 'Soup Queen of South Africa'. A large silver soup tureen was always standing on her dining table with some delicious soup she had cooked herself.

Having been introduced to her through the good offices of the Ramsays, she took a liking to me and invited me to her home one night for dinner.

The famous silver tureen stood on the table, and when I asked for a second helping of its contents, because I liked them so much, she became my friend for life.

I saw her quite often after this, and one day when I felt particularly depressed at being stuck in Johannesburg, she asked: 'What's the matter? Why so glum?'

I told her that although the English medical officer at our Calcutta base had checked me out as 'returning to the UK on medical grounds', the South African medics had decreed that I was fit enough to continue service in South Africa until the 'end of hostilities'. I confessed that I found my position as clerk at a military hospital somewhat humiliating; that I was no longer *in* the war, but wasn't out of it either.

'It's a most unsatisfactory state of affairs.'

'In that case we must see what we can do,' said Carrie. 'Cheer up, things aren't half as hopeless as you think.'

Two days later I was sent to have another medical – if you could call it that. It was like a scene out of a Gilbert and Sullivan opera.

Entering the office marked MO I saw two uniformed men sitting at a desk each, at opposite sides of the room, writing away. They took no notice of me. After a long pause, feeling an utter fool, I said: 'I've come for my medical.'

'Yes, you're having it now,' said one of them.

'Shall I undress?'

'No, just wait.'

So I stood there, waiting, and feeling more and more foolish by the minute. At last the one who had not yet spoken said: 'That's it! You're unfit for military service.'

'You're being posted back to the UK,' said the other, and with that they both gathered the papers on their desks, came over to me and handed me my documents. 'Good luck,' they said in unison and returned to their desks.

It took another six weeks before I was actually on the high seas again, bound for Britain.

From Johannesburg I was first posted back to the Clairwood transit camp, but soon received permission to stay with the Ramsays in Durban until the Dutch liner

New Amsterdam would be sailing for the U.K.

It was an extraordinary situation: here was I, an ordinary airman in the RAF, being treated as a VIP, living in style at the Ramsay's beautiful home – and a motorcycle rider calling there each week with my pay! I had no duties to perform; all I had to do was to relax and enjoy myself. Which I did.

The *New Amsterdam* finally sailed in the beginning of 1944 – two years after I had left home to 'go to war'.

We sailed without escort, zigzagging our way across the seas to avoid U-boats and enemy planes, and our voyage took months. All that time we never saw land.

The ship had a large number of troops on board; among them Australians and some Scottish units. Many were, like myself, being sent home for medical reasons. All of us were keenly aware of the danger we were in, sailing without protection against air attacks, or against being shot up by torpedos launched from an enemy warship or submarine.

One night, when I was sleeping out on deck, one of the Scottish lads came up to me: 'Sandy's afeared,' he said.

And now, to my joy, I heard the same voice that had comforted me on my voyage out: 'There's nothing to worry about, son,' it said. 'You'll get home safe and sound.'

Sandy was not the type of person I could tell about 'the voice'. That would have terrified him utterly; so I just said that somehow I felt we were safe and that nothing bad was going to happen to us.

He accepted that, and, comforted, bedded himself down beside me.

Our voyage was tedious in the extreme. Most of us were going home, yes, and we were looking forward to being back with our loved ones, but the buoyancy, the spirit of high adventure that had borne the troops out to war in the convoy of ships in 1942 was lacking.

Boredom spread like a disease and bored men get quarrelsome. The officers found it extremely difficult to maintain discipline. I kept myself very much to myself and steered clear of the ugly scenes that broke out every now and then.

I could always find a secluded spot somewhere on board and in long solitary hours I thought of all that had happened to me during the last two years. How I had been guided safely through the hardships and dangers of war; how I had never met up with any serious situation of 'kill or be killed' – shooting my rifle into the air had been the only warlike act ever required of me!

How at every turn I had met the right people at the right time; had received help when in trouble, expert medical attention when I needed it, and a fabulous operation that had cured my feet; finally, how, through the intervention of Carrie Rothkugel and the influence of Tom Ramsay, editor of South Africa's most important newspaper, I had been given the opportunity of returning home before the end of the war.

It puzzled me that I had been given such protection when so many young men and women had been killed, maimed, tortured, or taken prisoner, especially during the Burma campaign of which I had been a part! Why? I had no special talent to offer mankind and had certainly done nothing in the past to deserve such an easy ride through the hazards of war.

My psychic faculties had seemed dormant throughout that period; except for the reassuring voice I had heard on my way out from Britain and now again on my way back, I had had no signs from that 'other world'. Not from my sister, nor from my grandfather, John Upfold.

It took many years before I received the answer to my questions. In the meantime I could only hope that I would be guided in the future as I had been in the past.

My thoughts often raced ahead of time, anticipating my homecoming. I tried to imagine – to 'see' – Florence and little Alan at home; in vain. I got no image. They seemed wrapped in a dense grey cloud. I tried to intercept my mother's thoughts. We had always been so close that it should have been easy, but I was quite unable to make any mental contact. Well, I thought resignedly, telepathy obviously doesn't work with me.

I had had no news from home for many weeks before we sailed, but this time it didn't worry me. I'd been moved far too often for mail to catch up with all my postings.

Anyway, I'd be home soon now!

Chapter 4

Aftermath

Brighton! I took a deep breath as I stepped from the train onto the platform. I was back again – safe and sound, as I had been promised.

My heart beat faster as I walked along the familiar streets towards home. I had sent a telegram from Liverpool, where we had docked the day before, but hadn't been able to give my time of arrival in Brighton, as I didn't know how long formalities would take before I could get away. So, of course, there had been no one to meet me at the station.

I had been given a fortnight's home leave before I was to report to Tangmere aerodrome, where I would have to await my discharge from the RAF.

When I got to College Street, Kemptown, the street where we lived, I saw that it was filled with flags and bunting; a big streamer stretched across the road read: *Welcome Home, Tom.*

My neighbourhood was doing me proud! I felt happy and a little embarrassed.

Arriving at our door, I put my kitbag down and knocked. It opened, and there stood my son: 'You're my Dad,' he said, beaming up at me. 'I know, I know, you're my Dad!'

I picked him up in my arms and hugged and kissed him. He looked at me solemnly: 'Are you going to stay with us now?'

'Yes, Alan, I'm home and will be staying with you.'

Now neighbours were coming out to greet me and in a moment I was surrounded by people shaking my hands, wishing me 'welcome' and saying how delighted they were to have me back from the war all in one piece.

My mother appeared in the doorway, her eyes brimming with tears. Unable to speak, she just flung her arms round my neck and whispered into my ear:

'I'm so glad you're back, so very, very glad.'

And there was Florence! My heart gave a painful lurch as her eyes met mine. I could see no joy in them. She looked pale and thin and her shoulders drooped as if they were carrying a heavy burden.

I stepped up to her and folded her into my arms: 'It's all right, love, I'm back with you now. All's well.'

There was no response to my embrace. Her body felt limp. It was as if I held a ragdoll in my arms.

My mother, holding Alan by the hand, said: 'Let's get indoors.'

The neighbours melted away into their houses. I let go of Florence, picked up my bag and stepped into the house.

Never, as long as I live, will I be able to forget the time that followed my homecoming. Even now, after so many years, my heart grows cold as I remember.

That same night, when I tried with tenderness and gentle persuasion to make her open her heart to me, the whole pathetic story poured out of Florence – no longer my love, my wife, but a stranger, a distraught woman, who yet found the courage to tell the truth, hiding nothing.

It had begun with a harmless flirtation with a Canadian soldier, but had not stayed harmless for long. Passionate by nature, lonely and longing for tenderness, she had given way and started an affair with him.

'I fell in love, Tom.' Her face looked as if carved of stone as she said it. 'When I became pregnant he told me not to worry; that he loved me and would take me to

Canada after the war. I believed him and I wanted his child.'

That was over a year ago. The Canadian unit had moved away, and when the baby was born its father had already left. Florence never heard from him again.

The child died a few days after birth and in her despair Florence had turned to another, older man, who was helpful and kind. He had been her lover until, quite recently, he had confessed that he was a married man with two children, and had given her to understand that he would never leave his wife and family.

So that was it! Everything suddenly fell into place: my lack of news from home when I was in Burma, my being cut off from any contact with the spirit world – for what comfort could my sister, my grandfather, or any denizen of that world have given me? The truth had to remain hidden until I discovered it for myself; even my own inability to make any mental contact with my mother or Florence now made sense. My mother must have been in agony over the whole business and Florence had shut herself off from me. No wonder I 'saw' nothing but a blank, grey wall!

I remembered the warning my mother had given me in the early days of my friendship with Florence; how she had repeated it when she saw me falling deeper and deeper in love. Her words, made in a last attempt to prevent my taking the final step now rang in my ears: 'don't go through with this marriage; it'll go wrong if you do and she'll let you down in the end . . . you are not meant for each other.'

Those words had been spoken in 1932, and now, in 1944 – twelve years later – my mother's prediction had come true!

I fell into a state of uncomprehending despair. How could ten years of happily married life, of love and mutual joy and pride in our son be destroyed, be wiped out by two years of wartime separation?

That my story was not an unusual one, that it repeated itself endlessly in every war, was no consolation to me. The idea that Florence could forget the ties that bound us and fall in love with some other man had never occurred to me; even when I had worried myself sick over hearing nothing from home, *that* possibility had never entered my mind.

As far as I was concerned my life was shattered; had not all my plans for the future centred on Florence and our life together? Through all my war experiences – good and bad – she had never been far from my thoughts and never out of my heart.

I don't know what I would have done if my mother had not been around. With unending patience she explained, advised, consoled.

When I told her that I blamed myself for not listening to her warnings; that by marrying Florence I had probably ruined not only mine, but Florence's life as well, she said: 'No, Tom, no, it isn't like that at all! I warned you, because I could see that you and Florence did not belong together and that in the end you would both get hurt; but you had a perfect right to make your own choice. If it was the wrong choice life would rectify it – a painful process, but one from which lessons are to be learnt. How else do you think a human soul is made to grow and develop? And this goes for Florence just as much as for yourself.'

I was still cut off from contacts with the spirit world and couldn't understand why.

'Have you forgotten,' replied my mother, 'that the spirit world has laws, just as our world has, which have to be obeyed? There are times when a human soul on earth has to draw strength from its own inner resources, fight its own battles and rise up by its own efforts. In such cases no intervention from beyond is possible; and just think how unfair it would be if those psychic gifts could always call up spirit help, whilst other folk must flounder alone as best they can! Psychic gifts are bestowed primarily to help others – not ourselves.'

That sunk in. I accepted my mother's precepts and started to work my way out of hopelessness and depression.

It wasn't easy. I had loved Florence with all the passion

43

of a young and ardent heart. Our marriage had seemed inviolate. I had never doubted that Florence loved and needed me as much as I loved and needed her.

The shock of realising how different reality was to the idealistic picture I had carried in my heart, went deep; besides, my 'ego' was hurt and the sympathetic murmurings of friends and neighbours, who all knew what had happened, cut me to the quick.

Outwardly things moved rapidly. Florence had made no move towards a reconciliation and would not resist divorce proceedings.

I was too wrapped up in my own despair at the time, but later I realised how much she, too, must have suffered. She harboured no illusions about the possibility of saving our marriage. There was nothing left to save, and after a fortnight of sheer misery for all concerned she left our home and moved in with a woman friend who lived nearby.

It was the best solution, though I didn't like the fact that Florence insisted on taking Alan with her; but my solicitor calmed my misgivings: 'Never mind now. It won't be for long. The divorce will be through in no time, it's such a clear case, and you'll be granted custody of your son.'

That was exactly what happened. The divorce went through within weeks, I was given the custody of my boy, and the day after the court proceedings he was back: 'I've come to live with you, Dad,' he said simply after I had opened the front door to his knock. He marched upstairs, his arms full of toys, and re-possessed his room. Ten minutes later he was quietly at play. Sensible child!

He was five now and I wasn't very happy with his state of health. He looked peaky and was much too thin; quite unlike the bonny little boy I had left behind two years ago. The most worrying feature was that his chest was weak.

In the meantime I had taken up my duties at Tangmere aerodrome. There were, in fact, no duties for me to perform; I simply had to await my release papers.

Throughout this period the RAF gave me all the help and consideration I could possibly have wished for. I had a 'sleeping out pass', which meant that I could return home each night; when I told the CO about my worries over Alan's health, he had him examined by an RAF doctor, and on his recommendation he was sent to a convalescent home in North Devon, expenses paid by the RAF Benevolent Fund. After about two months he returned fit and well.

I was on full pay for the three months it took for my papers to come through, plus another four weeks after my final discharge.

The Co-op offered me my old job back and shortly after my demob papers had arrived, I was once again storekeeper in their pharmaceutical department.

Life gradually began to take on a semblance of normality. My mother presided over our small household with much common sense. She even taught me to cook.

'A man should be able to look after himself,' was her firm comment when I tried to get out of such unmanly domestic chores.

Alan settled down nicely when he came back from Devon. He didn't seem to pine after his mother. All his love went out to 'Granny' and 'Dad' and he was a joy to both of us.

There were no signs that he had inherited any psychic gifts and I couldn't make up my mind whether to be glad or sad about this. On the one hand I would have welcomed it if my son had carried on the 'psychic family tradition', on the other I knew that he would be spared much trouble, heartache, mockery and scorn if he lacked such gifts.

He remained unburdened by intrusions of that 'other world' into his daily life and consequently schooldays, which started soon after his return from Devon, were happy days for him – very different from mine!

The psychic faculties have not been passed on, but I'm content with things as they are, for Alan has made a success of his life and that is really all that matters.

As for myself, I had no contact with the spirit world for a long time. Today I know that it was a time of testing, of finding my own strength. I knew even then that I had to stand firm, that the way would be shown and that one day I would know the meaning of the lessons I was made to learn so painfully.

For the present, however, I was standing before locked doors. What was I to do with my life? I was back in my old job, yes, and I was grateful for the opportunity it gave me to get back to a normal, everyday life, but it was no permanent solution.

I had a long talk with my mother.

'Put your personal sorrow behind you, Tom,' she counselled. 'Forget the past and look to the future.'

'That's just what I'm trying to do,' I countered. 'I'd like to do something worthwhile, something of real use to mankind. There isn't much chance of doing anything positive and helpful in my present position.'

'Patience, darling! I can tell you one thing: your future is bright. You would not believe me when I predicted ill for your marriage – but I was right, wasn't I – so please believe me now when I predict a full life for you; a life of service and achievement.'

'What would you have me do?' I asked.

'Stay where you are and use every opportunity to render whatever service comes you way.'

It was really odd, but not long after that talk I began to meet a great number of sick or ailing people at work. Some were fellow workers, some customers, and among friends and relatives too I seemed to come up against all kinds of ills and complaints.

Tentatively at first, I took up the challenge and started healing. To my joy it worked, and at the same time, roughly three months after I'd started work at the Co-op, my contacts with the spirit world were restored.

All this brought me back to sanity. I began to take renewed interest in life, in my work – yes, even in my mundane storekeeper's duties – and, above all, in my attempts at healing. I achieved no great 'cures'; but I seemed to be able to give relief in painful conditions, remove headaches and often even speed recovery in more serious illnesses.

My mother was delighted. 'You're on the right road now,' she said. 'Mind you, your path won't always be an easy one. You'll suffer disappointments, rebuffs, scorn and disbelief. It won't be a bed of roses; but I also see success, true spiritual achievement and much happiness. Never lose heart, never give up – you will win through, and the greatest happiness will come to you through the one who is your "true love". You will meet her by and by, not for some time yet.'

There was one more sad blow in store for me: my mother's passing. Less than two years after my return she died of cancer.

I tended her at home as long as that was possible and it was only right at the end that she was taken to hospital.

'Dad is waiting for me, Tom,' she said. 'I'm glad to go.'

I missed her sorely, but didn't have long to wait before she showed herself: coming home one night, I saw her sitting on the top step of the staircase leading to the second floor, just as she had done so often during her life time, when she had finished cleaning the house.

Before she died she had looked frail and spent. Pain had etched deep lines into her face and her once large, luminous eyes had faded and grown dim. Now she looked her old self again; bright-eyed, happy and years younger.

After that I saw her often sitting up there on her favourite 'point of rest' as she had always called it; at other times I would find her sitting on the edge of my bed on waking in the morning; or she would appear when I had got into bed at night, particularly when I wasn't feeling well. On such occasions she would place her hand on my forehead, just as she had done when I was a child, and it would feel as cool and soothing as it had done then.

Sometimes my father would put in an appearance, but my most frequent visitor was my sister.

She used to chide me when she noticed that at times I was still thinking of Florence and still feeling hurt.

47

'You mustn't; really you mustn't,' she used to say, sounding quite cross, 'because all that lies behind you now and one day you will meet the right person – the one meant for you from the beginning.'

She couldn't or wouldn't tell me anything more; except that I should be patient and wait.

With time, Florence and all the bitterness connected with her memory did fade from my heart and mind. Many years later I heard that she had married again and hoped in all sincerity that she had found true happiness.

There was nothing for me to complain of now: I had a safe job with the Co-op, which gave me a decent living, I did some healing in the evening after work and during weekends, saw friends, enjoyed occasional visits to the theatre – and slowly but surely began to feel dissatisfied. My life seemed to have become stuck in a groove.

Then, in 1946, something happened that cleared away all doubts as to what I was to do with my life.

I had decided one fine summer's morning to rise very early to go and collect a longstanding debt from a client. It was close on 7 am when I was walking up Egremont Place – a very ordinary Brighton street. Usually full of traffic, even at that early hour, it was strangely quiet that morning. No cars, no people; not a soul to be seen anywhere.

All of a sudden I heard a voice calling my name. Surprised, I stopped and looked around. Nobody there. The street was as empty as before. I carried on, feeling a little uneasy, and again it called. Louder this time: 'Tom Pilgrim!' I stopped dead and looked up to see if someone was calling from a window.

There was no one; but high above the houses, outlined against a clear blue sky, I saw a huge cross, the colour of burnished gold, gleaming in the early morning sunlight. It was exquisite! I blinked and rubbed my eyes: the cross remained. It stood in the motionless air as if sculpted; so solid you thought you could climb up it.

I stood on the pavement, quite still and looked up at the cross until it started to vanish – slowly, from the base upwards.

It was impossible to feel or act normally after such an experience. I made a futile attempt at calling on the person I had set out to see. Luckily he wasn't in. I'm sure I would have talked gibberish if I had met him. By the time I arrived at work I had somewhat gathered my wits, but I was no good that day. Why has this happened to me, I kept thinking? What does it mean? I'm not a religious man, never have been!

Trying to find an answer, I went to St Anne's Church every evening at 7 o'clock for a week; sitting quietly, always in the sixth pew from the front, I waited for a sign. None came.

In desperation I went to see the vicar, half expecting him to doubt my word. He said he believed me but couldn't answer my question. He looked earnestly at me: 'I wish it had happened to me, Mr Pilgrim! That is all I can say.'

About three months later, lying in bed one night reading a book, I looked up and saw a man standing at the foot of my bed, watching me. I knew instantly that this man was connected with the golden cross I had seen, and in a flash I understood that the cross was a symbol of the work I was to undertake.

I wanted to ask a thousand questions of this man at the foot of my bed, but couldn't bring out a single word. He looked at me without breaking his silence and then slowly vanished.

After two months he appeared again, and this time he spoke. He had been a doctor in his earth life, he told me, was continuing his work in the spirit world, and would like to use me as his medium when the time was ripe. He gave his name as Dr Robert Koch and aware of the fact that I couldn't understand his surname, spelled it out for me.

I felt an upsurge of deep joy. So it was true – healing was to be my life's vocation!

For some time after this nothing out of the ordinary

happened. I went on healing as before, in the evenings after work and on holidays and weekends; but, instead of just 'feeling' the presence of spirit entities when I was healing, I could now at times 'see' this Dr Robert Koch. His surname foxed me, so I decided to call him simply 'Dr Robert'.

Confirmation of the truth of these strange experiences came when I developed a stomach ulcer and decided, after twelve months of agony and unsuccessful orthodox medical treatment, to consult J J Thomas, then a famous spiritualist healer.

J J Thomas went into a deep trance – as he always did when healing – and the spirit entity who came through to treat me was none other than Dr Robert!

He thumped my tummy and said: 'No good. I'm going to take this ulcer out. It will take twenty minutes. Do you want to talk?'

'Yes,' I answered, and whilst he was operating, he told me the story of my life from childhood to that day.

'We know more about you than you know yourself,' he commented.

'Spirit operations' are performed on the etheric counterpart of the physical body; they take place in a different dimension, and so you never feel any pain when the actual operation is carried out; but the results are transferred to the physical body, which has to 'catch up' as it were and that is a process you may feel.

'Tomorrow you may have much pain,' said Dr Robert when the operation was over; 'but don't regret having come here. When you're in pain, just call me. Say: "help me, Dr Robert", and I shall be there. The pain will become less each day and at the end of a week you'll be cured. I'm leaving now. Speak to my medium.'

Mr Thomas came out of trance, an astonished expression on his face: 'You are going to do this work yourself one day,' he said.

My cure happened exactly as Dr Robert had foretold. After a week of intermittent spasms of pain and frequent calls for help, which Dr Robert always answered, I was fine. When I went back to my ordinary doctor, and X-rays

showed that my ulcer had disappeared, he was astoun-
ded.

'It was a large, serious ulcer! How come it is no longer
there?' he asked in great puzzlement; but he was an open-
minded man, and when I told him I had been to see a
spiritual healer he said: 'Good for you!'

The other prediction also came true: round about
1960, after J J Thomas had passed on, I became Dr
Robert's medium.

In the beginning I used to go into trance when Dr
Robert took over, just as Thomas had done; but I didn't
like it. I wanted to know what was going on and what
was being said, which of course I couldn't, being in deep
trance. When I asked Dr Robert what I could do about it,
he advised me to have some music playing during the
healing.

'Music will act as a kind of "anchor" to your
consciousness, preventing it from being blotted out
completely; it will be dimmed whilst I'm taking over, but
you'll be aware of what's happening.'

It's a method that works very well for me and I've been
using it for many years now; but if for any reason I treat a
patient without music – off I go into a trance.

A long time was to pass before I learnt the true identity
of my 'Dr Robert'.

In 1979 a journalist asked me in the course of an
interview: 'You refer to the spirit entity who heals
through you always as 'Dr Robert'. Is that his first name
or his surname?'

'His first name,' I told her, and went on to explain that
I could not pronounce his surname correctly and had
therefore always been reluctant to use it. I also told her
how he had once spelled it out for me: 'K-o-c-h'.

'Dr Robert Koch!' exclaimed the journalist. 'There
was a famous German doctor and scientist of that name,
who received the Nobel Prize for medicine early this
century.'

Well, I had to admit my ignorance. I didn't have a clue.
The history of medicine – and German medical history at
that – is a book with seven seals to me.

'Could you give me any details about your Dr Robert?' the journalist enquired excitedly. 'It would be quite a story if it really were "the" Dr Robert Koch!'

I could now 'see' Dr Robert. He had appeared whilst we were talking and was standing near the journalist, a highly amused expression on his face.

'I'll be glad to help you,' I heard him say.

Turning to the journalist, I told her that Dr Robert was present, that I could 'see' and 'hear' him and that he was willing to give us some dates.

Being used to interviewing mediums, she accepted this quite naturally; so I took up a block of notepaper and wrote down what Dr Robert told me:

His birthplace sounded like 'Clausweil'; I got the 'Claus' quite clearly, then 'wal' or 'weil'. He said he was born in 1843; became Doctor of Medicine in 1866 (I had trouble understanding the '66' and had to ask twice); 1870–71 he served as a medical officer in the Franco-Prussian war; 1876 he was given an important post in the Ministry of Health in Berlin; 1882 he discovered the tuberculosis bacillus, and in 1905 received the Nobel Prize for medicine. He died in Baden-Baden, Germany, in 1910.

I tore the page off the block and handed it to the journalist.

Next day the telephone rang. The journalist was on the line from London: 'I compared the notes you wrote down with those relating to Dr Robert Koch in a German encyclopaedia. They are correct, and his birthplace is given as "Clausthal". Your Dr Robert really is the famous German scientist Dr Robert Koch!'

I was a little overwhelmed by this revelation but Dr Robert's comment was brief: 'What I did on earth has become unimportant. It lies in the past. All that matters now is the work that you and I are doing together.'

Chapter 5

A New Beginning

From the moment Dr Robert had made himself known to me, my life changed. That is, outwardly it remained much the same: I continued with my job at the Co-op and healed in my spare time, but everything I did seemed to take on a new meaning. I had found my purpose in life and consequently the dissatisfaction and restlessness that had plagued me disappeared.

It was replaced by a quiet resolve to make the best use of every opportunity to do healing; to get as much experience as possible and, above all, to prove myself worthy of the great service entrusted to me.

I had to be careful in my approach to patients in those early days; I was, after all, an 'unknown quantity' and had to win their confidence.

In the beginning, when I noticed that a person I met at work, or in my spare time, had some kind of ailment, I always waited until a remark was made about it. I would then show interest and carefully bring the conversation round to spiritual healing; if I found that the person concerned had an open mind on the subject I would offer help, but would never promise results. The results, however, were forthcoming and by and by I became quite well known in Brighton.

One of the first really remarkable healing successes I, or to be more correct, Dr Robert achieved, was with a man desperately ill with leukaemia.

This particular person, who shall remain nameless, was a real ne'er-do-well; a materialist, who didn't believe in anything 'spiritual' whatsoever. It was through his wife, who turned to me as a last resort, that I got to know of this case. According to medical opinion there was no hope. Hospital treatment had been discontinued.

For two months I went to his home regularly twice a week to give him healing. He submitted to it without enthusiasm, not believing for a moment that it could work.

One evening, when I placed my hands on him to give the usual five to ten minutes healing, I felt an odd burning sensation in my fingertips and when I withdrew my hands I saw that I had a large black blister on the tip of each finger. Painful they were too!

'I'm drawing out the bad blood and replacing it by a fresh supply,' I heard Dr Robert say. 'The blisters are caused by the bad blood. Don't worry, they'll disappear again quite quickly.' Which, thank God, they did.

This was the turning point. From that day on the patient improved rapidly until a complete cure was achieved.

It caused a sensation! The doctors at the hospital were non-plussed. At the time – it happened over twenty-five years ago – no effective medical treatment for leukaemia was known. Patients always died sooner or later.

I can no longer remember the exact conclusions the medics at the hospital drew from this case, but they certainly did not accept that the cure was due to 'spiritual healing'.

Today many doctors have an open mind and accept at least the possibility of spirit healing, and an ever increasing number of hospitals allow psychic healers to visit patients; but at the time medical opinion – with rare exceptions – rejected any ideas that lay outside the concepts of orthodox medicine.

As far as I remember the hospital authorities' final verdict was that my patient's cure was due to 'remission'. Whatever that may have meant, the man is still alive today, enjoying a healthy old age.

Two aspects of this case are of special interest: firstly, it proves that 'spiritual' or 'psychic' healing has nothing to do with 'faith'. The patient in question was an atheist who had no faith at all. I have had many similar cases in my long healing career; in healing babies, for instance, where the question of 'faith' simply doesn't arise, and I always resist being called a 'faith healer' because it is an incorrect label, a misnomer.

Healing is given to good and bad alike, and herein lies the other important point of this cure. The man healed was, as already mentioned, a materialist who never aspired to anything higher in life than the satisfaction of his own, selfish desires. The healing he received did not touch his heart or open up his soul. He remained the egotistic rogue he had always been.

Therefore, from a spiritual point of view, the cure was but a partial success. The healing of the body is only one aspect; the other, perhaps even more important aim of a cure is to touch the soul of the patient, so that the result of the healing will bring an awareness of the reality of spiritual values. That did not happen in this case.

It is a very affecting moment for a healer when a patient, realising that he or she has been healed when all hope seemed lost, recognises the power of the spirit and is moved to tears by the powerful emotion this evokes. Such cases are the perfect ones, because both objects, the physical and the spiritual, have been achieved.

The leukaemia case fell into the period before I actually became Dr Robert's permanent medium. It was, in a way, a time of apprenticeship. Dr Robert Koch was preparing me for the day when I would have to take over as his medium from J J Thomas.

That day came in 1960, after Dr Robert's first medium had died. Just as J J Thomas had done, I now started to go into trance whenever Dr Robert took over completely, which happened more and more often as time went on. Patients were a bit startled at first, but when I gave them an explanation of trance conditions and made it clear to them that Dr Robert was really the healer and I only his instrument, they accepted this new development and soon got used to it.

The number of patients grew steadily and my life was a

full one indeed, what with the work at the Co-op and healing sessions in my spare time. I never accepted any fees for healing in those days; earning a decent living at the Co-op, I didn't feel entitled to take money for the use of my gift of healing. Even now, as a fulltime healer, I make no charges. Patients are left entirely free to give whatever they like.

The traumatic experience of my marriage break-up had left me, as far as my personal, intimate life was concerned, lonely and withdrawn. I became more and more a 'man's man' who liked the company of his pals. A drink at the pub, evenings at the theatre – I had a soft spot for variety shows – football and cricket matches and an occasional visit to the races were the relaxations I enjoyed.

'The greatest happiness will come to you through the one who is your "true love". You will meet her by and by, but not for some time yet,' my mother had told me in 1944, at the height of my despair over the loss of Florence.

Once again she proved right: twenty-three years later, in 1967, I met the woman who, without doubt, was 'meant for me'.

I had become deeply interested in Spiritualism and often visited a Spiritualist church in Brighton. Services at Spiritualist churches usually include a demonstration of clairvoyance and clairaudience by a medium. This always fascinated me, because, as I myself could 'see' and 'hear' spirit entities, I always knew when so-called 'spirit messages' were genuine and when they were not.

One day, after the service, I got talking to the lady who had been sitting next to me. We discussed the medium and the messages he had given, and I was struck by the sound knowledge this lady seemed to have of mediumship, its difficulties and pitfalls.

It turned out that she herself had strong psychic faculties and that she stemmed from a highly mediumistic family. Her grandmother had been psychic and had passed on her gifts to her children and grandchildren.

56

After this first encounter we always had lengthy chats whenever we met at a Spiritualist church service. On one such occasion Phyllis – that was my new friend's name – told me about some tapes she had, which demonstrated the 'direct voice' phenomenon. The 'direct voice' is a very rare psychic phenomenon in which, through a complicated process, spirit entities project their voices 'direct', that is from *outside* a deeply entranced medium.

My excitement at what she was telling me must have shown in my face, for she asked rather shyly. 'Would you like to hear the tapes?'

'Oh yes, very much,' I answered, 'I have never heard a "direct voice".'

So I was invited to Phyllis' home, a guesthouse which she ran with the help of her sister-in-law, and where her widowed mother also lived.

Listening to the tapes was certainly exciting; but to watch Phyllis move about in her own home environment was a much more thrilling experience. I suddenly became conscious of her loveliness. I knew she was a woman somewhere in her forties, for she had told me that she, like her sister-in-law, was a widow and that she had a grown-up son; but with her trim figure and graceful movements, her soft brown hair and grey-blue eyes that shone with good humour, she looked years younger than her age.

For the first time in more than twenty years I had met a woman who could make my heart beat faster.

We started going out together, and when we discovered that we shared an equal interest in the theatre, we made a habit of seeing any worthwhile show that appeared in Brighton.

It was no whirlwind courtship – we were both mature people, no longer prone to youthful ecstasies, but slowly, almost imperceptively, we grew into each other's lives until one could not do without the other.

We had wonderful times together, sometimes going over to France on day-trips, exploring Calais, Dieppe, or Boulogne. On Sundays, unless we were away, I was always at Phyllis' home for lunch or dinner.

Our greatest bond was Spiritualism. Endless hours were spent in discussions, in which Phyllis' mother and sister-in-law would join eagerly.

Spiritual healing was probably the subject that came up most often and we discovered that when I was treating the leukaemia case – many years ago – Phyllis had heard about it through the sick man's mother, who had been a neighbour at the time.

'My son has only six months to live,' she had said to Phyllis one day, and later: 'Just fancy, my son is being treated by a psychic healer and is improving. He is not going to die!'

Phyllis remembered how impressed she had been by this 'healing miracle'.

On Christmas Day in 1968 Phyllis had to be with relatives in Ipswich – the whole family was going – but she was determined to be with me on New Year's Eve. So back she came for the 31st of Decembr, and I was invited to dinner at her home. We had a lovely meal together, with wine and all the festive trimmings.

I hardly dare relate what happened next, because, from Phyllis' point of view, I dropped such a horrendous brick that I'm surprised she ever forgave me: I left her long before midnight and went home to do my 'absent healing'. I always have a list of patients who receive 'absent healing', either in addition to contact healing, or because, for one reason or another, it is not possible for them to come and see me, nor for me to visit them. I call on Dr Robert and together we go through the names on the list, Dr Robert sending out 'healing rays' to each patient.

I had, as often happens, an inordinately long list of names that night, and I knew it would take me many hours to get through it.

'Phyl, darling,' I announced around 10 pm, 'I've got to go home now to do my absent healing.'

I'll never forget the expression of stark disbelief that spread across her face as I said it.

'But you can't,' she got out after a stunned silence. 'It's New Year's Eve, remember? We were going to see the new year in together!'

Of course I didn't want to go, but I thought it was my duty. Not going would have meant breaking faith with my patients, for I knew that if I stayed until after midnight I'd never get through my list.

So I went, and Phyllis, being the level headed, self-controlled person that she is, made no fuss, no scene; but there was a distinct coldness in her bearing the next time we met.

'There I was, alone in the house, facing the start of the new year all by myself. The man for whom I had travelled back from Ipswich, so that we could celebrate New Year's Eve together, having left me at ten o'clock,' she complained, when I tried, very gingerly, to apologise.

I must have looked terribly crestfallen, because suddenly her innate sense of humour got the upper hand and she burst out laughing.

'What a boyfriend to have, to be sure! I must admit that I was very upset at the time, but what an absurd situation – farcical enough to feature in a modern comedy!'

With that she flung her arms around me and said 'For heavens sake! Drop that hangdog expression – you're forgiven!'

We've often laughed about this incident in the years that followed. In fact, my absent healing can still cause problems when we're out, or away on one of my healing demonstration tours, and sometimes, when I start on my list very late, the whole night has gone before I'm through; but since I've become a fulltime healer my appointments are arranged in such a way that I can catch up with sleep during the day if necessary.

In January 1969 Connie, Phyllis' sister-in-law, died. This was a terrible blow for the whole family and particularly for Phyllis, who had been very close to her.

I too had been fond of Connie; she, Phyllis and I had so often, usually on Sundays, sat together talking about life after death and the philosophy of Spiritualism. Connie had been psychic to a certain extent herself, and quite aware of the spirit world surrounding us; so I wasn't at all surprised to 'see' Connie at her own funeral – smiling and serene and accompanied by a young man. Though I could describe him in detail, no one recognised him as a relative or friend who had passed on earlier. Perhaps he was a 'guide', helping her to adjust to her new state of being.

Connie's death caused a great upheaval in Phyllis' life. She lost all interest in the guesthouse she and Connie had run together and started thinking about selling it.

This was the right moment for me. I had known for some time now that Phyllis was my 'true love' and whenever my mother or my sister appeared, they confirmed that it was indeed so.

Phyl's grief had brought us very close together and when I asked her if she would marry me, I saw the first ray of happiness in her eyes since Connie's passing.

'Yes,' she said simply and then told me that she, too, was sure that we had been destined for each other. She knew the whole story of my first marriage, and in the long years since our first meeting her constant love and companionship has made up for every bit of misery I had suffered.

Phyllis could easily have become a successful medium in her own right. In the 1950s she had done a great deal of 'automatic writing' with highly interesting results (the hand of the writer is guided by a spirit entity in automatic writing). Later she started to develop trance-mediumship; but she has laid aside all her personal aspirations and has devoted her whole life to helping me in my healing mission.

A healer's life is strenuous. Much energy is expended in the healing process; vitality and strength have to be husbanded, or the healer will become drained of vital forces and his health, and with that his work will suffer.

Phyllis takes all the administrative worries off my shoulders, answers the phone, makes the appointments, receives the patients and shields me from unannounced callers; she helps me to deal with the massive mail I receive from all over the world, and is with me at public demonstrations at home and abroad; her own deep knowledge of psychic matters is, of course, a constant help in many ways.

We married in June 1969 and Phyllis, having sold her guesthouse, moved to my place together with her mother.

Thereby hangs another, rather unusual, tale: apart from a weekend alone in London after our wedding, Phyl's mother shared our honeymoon! Just as in the pop song 'And her mother came too . . .' she went with us for our fortnight's stay in Devon.

We lived very happily in my old home in College Street for about a year; but in 1970 we found a semi-detached house in Patcham, another Brighton district, which suited us better. I left the Co-op, and after Phyllis' mother had died (her room was turned into my first real healing sanctuary), I was able to take up healing full time.

No doubt my marriage to Phyllis was the most important turning point of my life.

My days became organised and geared to one aim: the healing of the sick and the alleviation of suffering.

The 'divine plan', as my mother had foretold, was fulfilling itself. Material worries, so much a part of my early life, were no longer a problem. The money Phyllis had inherited from her mother, plus that which the sale of the guesthouse had brought in, gave us a firm financial starting basis.

That my life had indeed been planned and guided was confirmed when Phyllis and I were invited to a sitting of the 'Hannen Swaffer Home Circle' in 1977. This circle had been started in 1934 by Hannen Swaffer, the famous journalist who had been known as the 'Pope of Fleet Street' and Maurice Barbanell, editor of the Spiritualist weekly *Psychic News* and the monthly journal *Two Worlds* until his sudden death in July 1981. Barbanell was the medium of 'Silver Birch', a spirit being who became famous in Spiritualist circles – and beyond – for the addresses he gave during the sittings at Barbanell's

London home. Through his deeply entranced medium, Silver Birch woud counsel, teach and lecture; shedding light on human problems, giving advice and expounding the philosophy of spirit truths.

'You are spirits with a body, not bodies with a spirit – you always "were" and always will "be",' was one of his favourite sayings.

He would address each visitor to his circle individually, making him or her feel immediately at ease.

'I do not have to tell you or your wife that all that has happened is part of a plan,' he said, turning to me. 'You are richly blessed. You have been led to your partner because she was necessary to the work that you do together. All that has happened is part of this plan, not only for you, but for the world in which you live, because those who have any gift of the spirit have a vital part to play.'

He said much to both of us that was of great impact and finally he asked me if I had a question.

'Yes,' I answered. 'It has been said to me that I asked to be born a healer. How would that come about? Could you explain that a little to me?'

'I will try,' responded Silver Birch. 'Some of you, before you incarnate into your world, realising what lies in front of you, make a choice as to what service you can render. This has to be done in consonance with evolved beings in our world. I call them the hierarchy, others refer to them as the masters. They are, if you like, those whose task it is to interpret the Great Spirit's wisdom and ensure that divine plans will always be fulfilled.

'You chose the healing, knowing that before awareness came, your path would be difficult, dark and, if I may be very frank, almost tragic.'

Remembering the war and the agony its aftermath had brought me, I could only admit that I had, indeed, suffered deeply.

'The essence of healing is compassion,' Silver Birch continued; 'unless you have compassion you cannot heal in a spiritual sense. Compassion is one of the spiritual attributes. In order to feel compassion for those who

62

suffer you have to suffer yourself. It is an essential ingredient in any medium's unfoldment.

'You made the choice; are you sorry?'

'Oh no, Silver Birch!' I said with conviction.

'You are both very richly blessed,' he concluded. 'Every morning when you wake your heart should sing with joy for the opportunities the new day will provide of giving a service none other can render.'

We had been installed in our Patcham home a little over a year, when a series of events started that led up to Dr Robert giving a lecture at London's famous Guy's Hospital.

One day, during the course of a routine dental treatment, my dentist came upon a tender spot on the gums of my lower jaw. X-rays revealed a large cyst.

'I'm sorry, but I can't deal with this,' said the dentist. 'You'll have to see the dental surgeon at the hospital.'

At the Sussex County Hospital, Brighton, the dental surgeon decided that an operation was needed.

'We'll have to break your jaw to get at this cyst,' he said. 'It's enormous!'

X-rays showed that it reached from just below my left ear to the middle of my chin.

'Break my jaw!' I exclaimed, horrified. 'How is it going to be put together again?'

'Nothing to worry about,' soothed the surgeon, 'your jaw will be wired up after the operation. You'll have a few weeks of discomfort whilst it's healing, but then you'll be as right as rain.'

I didn't like the sound of it at all. What if my jaw wouldn't knit together again?

No. I refused to submit to such an ordeal without at least getting a second opinion, and after some argument with my dentist, who said that I'd already had two opinions, his and the County Sussex Hospital's, I was sent to Guy's Hospital, London.

I was seen by Mr O'Driscoll, the head dental surgeon, a

charming man with a pronounced sense of humour.

'My word,' he said, scanning the latest crop of X-rays, 'what a whopper! It's the largest cyst ever – fit for the Guinness Book of Records!'

He disagreed with his Sussex colleague's intention of breaking my jaw.

'Nonsense,' he said, 'we'll get that villain out of your jaw without breaking any bones.'

He couldn't understand why I hadn't had any pain.

'Look, you must have had this damned thing for years; you're a most interesting case. Would you agree to come here a few times before we tackle your problem and be our "exhibit No 1"? I would like to give four lectures. Three to my students, and one to my dental surgery colleagues.'

I agreed and sat, feeling a little foolish, in the dental chair, whilst O'Driscoll lectured, showed X-rays and answered his students' questions.

During the last of these lectures, the one at which the doyens of dental surgery were present, I suddenly became very drowsy and felt myself nodding off. I tried to pull myself together, but it was no good; I fell asleep, or thought I did.

I awoke with a start, to find that everybody in the lecture room was staring at me. Thoroughly ashamed of myself I started to mumble my excuses.

'My dear fellow,' O'Driscoll's face showed a mingled expression of disbelief and sheer admiration, 'don't apologise; you weren't "asleep", you were in some sort of a trance and gave us a riveting twenty minute discourse on healing in general and this cyst of yours in particular.'

It had, of course, been Dr Robert, who had taken this opportunity to address his medical colleagues at Guys!

As my wife and I left the room and walked down the corridor on our way out, one of the dental surgeons came running after us.

'Mr Pilgrim,' he said when he had caught up with

Phyllis and me, 'that was the most wonderful lecture I ever heard.'

'Well, I know nothing about it,' I answered; 'it wasn't me talking.'

'Amazing! Now, can you tell me where I can get books on the subject,' he queried. 'I'm a complete ignoramus in these matters.'

'Yes, go to the Psychic Book Shop, 23 Great Queen Street, Holborn in London,' I said, 'they'll be glad to help you.'

'Thanks very much, I'll certainly do that. It's about time I learned about such things.'

We shook hands and went our separate ways.

'Nice bit of propaganda our Dr Robert did there,' remarked Phyllis.

The four lectures had been spread over some weeks and on the trips to London I had been reading a book Phyllis' brother had given me: *The Healing Touch*, by M H Tester, a Spiritual healer of repute, who lived not far from us, in Haywards Heath, Sussex.

I was very impressed by his book and decided to consult him about my cyst. Dr Robert didn't mind; 'It'll be an interesting experiment,' he said when I asked his advice.

So off I went, as one healer to another. Tester was then already well established and highly successful; he had started his mission after he himself had been healed of a spine ailment which might have led to a life in a wheelchair.

I felt the power emanating from his fingers stream into my jaw and noticed a prickly, stabbing sensation around the jaw bone.

The cyst had no doubt been loosened by Tester's treatment, but surgery was still necessary, and once more I presented myself at Guy's Hospital. This time for the operation.

I refused to have a general anaesthetic – I was much too interested in what was going to be done to me. O'Driscoll agreed to let me watch the whole procedure.

'As far as you're concerned, it's all done by mirrors,' he

joked, and gave me a local anaesthetic.

With the help of mirrors I could watch everything. It was fascinating.

After my gum had been cut open, the cyst was pulled out with the aid of very long forceps. It came out in bits, which O'Driscoll placed on a piece of black velvet cloth. They shone like diamonds!

'You see,' he said, 'the crystallisation shows the age of that cyst. About time it came out, it could have poisoned your whole system, and I'm surprised it hasn't done so already. It must have been growing apace in that jaw of yours for about thirty years!'

When I got back to Brighton, with Phyllis at my side, I began to feel a bit whoozy. The anaesthetic had worn off and pain was setting in; but the moment we walked out of the station a car came by, stopped, and a man poked his head out of the window.

'Hey, Tom!' he shouted.

It was an old pal of mine.

'You look as white as a sheet, and your jaw's all swollen; what's happened to you?'

On hearing my story he said 'Come on, jump in and I'll drive you home.'

My troubles were over. The jaw healed within a month and my energy, which had waned considerably during the last few months, renewed itself remarkably quickly.

When I tell friends about this strange experience they often ask: 'Why couldn't your Dr Robert prevent the cyst growing in the first place, or get it out by a "spirit operation"?'

The answer is simple: healers and mediums are by no means immune against 'the slings and arrows of outrageous fortune'; it would be most unfair if they were. Besides, did my cyst not serve a very good purpose? Did it not give Dr Robert the opportunity to give a lecture on psychic healing to a roomful of orthodox medical men? It must have set at least a few of them thinking, as was proved by the surgeon who asked for information on psychic subjects.

It may seem a rather odd service that I rendered by

producing this super cyst – but, to the surgeon's amazement, I had been kept clear of pain through all the years it had been growing.

That proves to me that Dr Robert had been watching over me, and that even the cyst happened 'according to plan'.

Chapter 6

Full Time Healing

My connection with the healer M H Tester was to prove a great help to me. We kept in touch over the 'cyst ordeal' and when Tester asked me if I would help with patients that came to his beautiful Haywards Heath home, I readily agreed.

For two years, from 1972 to 1974, I went over to Haywards Heath every Monday afternoon to share in the healing of Tester's many patients. We worked very well together, but my Brighton practice was growing rapidly, and after two years I could no longer afford the time for my weekly travels to Haywards Heath, so our joint healing efforts came to an end.

It had been an interesting venture from which, I think, we both profited. We stayed in contact with each other, and later, when Phyllis and I had moved to a house in Hove and discovered that it was riddled with damp, we received great kindness from Tester and his wife Jean, who invited us to stay with them until the trouble was put right.

Over the years a faithful little band of helpers has rallied round Phyllis and me – all of them patients who were cured and wanted to give some kind of service in return. They help with the reception of patients, the answering of mail, or give Phyllis a hand with household chores on special occasions. Their services are much appreciated.

Mrs Barbara Salmon was the first. She came to my Patcham sanctuary in 1972, sixty years of age and crippled with arthritis. She had to climb the stairs up to my sanctuary on the second floor and did it literally on all fours!

As a young girl and young married woman her health had been fine; but soon after the birth of her first baby it began to fail. It deteriorated slowly but steadily. At one point a hiatus hernia was diagnosed, and arthritis was eating into every joint in her body; by 1962 she had become a complete cripple, hobbling about painfully on two sticks. The usual treatments – she attended the Royal Sussex Hospital, Brighton – had no effect. Physiotherapy seemed to make things worse, not better. She had been very happily married to a devoted husband until, in 1972, he had suddenly died of a heart attack. Two loving daughters did their best to look after her, and it was one of her son-in-laws who told her about spiritual healing. Orthodox medicine had washed its hands of her: 'You'll have to learn to live with it,' had been the final verdict.

But Barbara Salmon is a very special person. She never threw up the sponge, never indulged in self pity and, as her daughters told me, insisted on as much independence as she could possibly maintain. What's more, she always tried to help others, realising that 'there's always someone even worse off than oneself'.

Up at the hospital she would encourage the other patients, filling even the most timid and fearful of souls with confidence and hope.

During one of her longer stays a fellow patient, a lady with an open sore on her forehead, was in a particularly low state of mind. The wound simply wouldn't heal and doctors and nurses were at a loss about what to do to help her.

Barbara sat down at her bedside and talked to her for a long time. The distraught patient slept peacefully that night and next morning, when the bandage was removed from her forehead, the nurse was delighted to find that the wound had stopped weeping.

Well, I'm glad to say that Barbara Salmon has been completely cured. She came for healing once a fortnight over a period of six months, improving with each visit.

'The first time I came to you,' she told me later, 'I felt calm and relaxed the moment you placed your hands on my body. I felt immediately that I was going to improve.'

Then, later still, when a complete cure had been achieved: 'Tom, it's like a miracle! After so many years of agonising pain and wretched immobility, I'm a normal, healthy person. I can walk, run, skip, jump – even climb ladders!'

She has regained the independence she values so much – no longer living with one of her daughters, but having a flat of her own, which she proudly redecorated all by herself.

To those who ask so often: 'but are these cures really permanent?' I can only answer: 'Barbara Salmon is as fit and well today, in 1981, as she was after her completed cure in 1973; even her hiatus hernia has been kept under control. She has had no troubles, no relapses.'

Requests for 'absent healing' come in from all over the world. Each request is answered and I always ask patients to report on their progress – or lack of it. Then there are the letters I receive from patients who come for contact healing and report on improvements between appointments.

'Reading those letters is an experience in itself!' says Gwendoline Hutchinson, who acts as a part-time secretary, typing out my answers.

She is always shaken by the flood of misery that lands on my desk: the pathetic stories of years of ill health, mental and physical distress, the hopes, fears, and sometimes the downright despair.

Gwendoline came to me in 1978, aged sixty, without hope, having suffered from migraine since childhood.

'I was thirteen when it started, and it ruined my life,' she told me. 'As a youngster I often had to miss school; I would wake up of a morning with a blinding headache and vomit every quarter of an hour. Staying in bed in a darkened room was the only way to combat those onslaughts. Attacks could last for three or four days. There seemed to be no cure; nothing tried by orthodox medicine worked.'

She married a successful businessman who surrounded her with never failing, loving care. She has two children and, strangely, during her pregnancies the migraine attacks stopped – only to return with renewed force once the child was born.

'It has been so difficult!' Gwendoline continued her report, 'My husband has his social obligations and I know how important it is for his work to honour them; yet, how often did he have to cancel a visit or an invitation, because I lay prostrate with one of my migraine attacks. He has taken me to see specialists and I've swallowed all the known drugs – nothing helps.'

She expected nothing that first time she came to see me. A friend had counselled her to try psychic healing, and she had read an article about my work in the spiritualist journal *Two Worlds*.

'I decided to come to you as a last resort,' she said on entering the sanctuary.

She was cured in a single sitting.

'Tom, it was the most sensational happening,' she confided later, when she offered her help as a 'small, a very small token of gratitude to you and Dr Robert.

'I can't really describe what I felt when I sat down and the healing took place. You switched on a tape of music and then came over to me. I couldn't see you, because I had closed my eyes; but when your hands lay on my head – one on my forehead, the other at the back of my head – it was as if some tremendous benevolent power enveloped me from the top of my head to the tips of my toes. Elation, and a feeling of well-being such as I had never known before swept over me. When the music stopped and you withdrew your hands, I sat motionless for a few seconds. Opening my eyes I saw you standing at the washbasin, washing your hands. You turned, smiled, and said "that's it! Dr Robert says you're cured. No more migraines." The relief I felt was unbelievable.'

If there's one thing that I've learnt since my work with Dr Robert started, it's that he never makes a promise he can't keep, and so I knew that Gwendoline's problem had been solved for good. From that day to this she hasn't had even a hint of migraine.

'You know,' she said one day to Phyllis and me over a cup of tea, 'the healing I received has had all sorts of side-effects! I had read books on Spiritualism before I met you, but I was a terrible sceptic; I didn't really believe what I read. Having had a rather strict Church of England upbringing, I was wearing blinkers. Anything outside the orthodox teachings seemed suspect! The healing has removed the blinkers and opened my eyes to the reality of the spirit world. That's another thing Dr Robert has done for me!'

Gwendoline's husband came to me for treatment when he developed back trouble; he too was cured, but he had to come several times. Cures achieved in a single sitting are comparatively rare, so Dr Robert is particularly pleased when they happen.

I must admit that I really have no idea why some people are healed instantly and others only after a shorter or longer period of time. Dr Robert has never explained it to me; but from the little he has told me, I understand that it depends not only on the disease or ailment, but also on the person to be treated.

Not all patients can be cured. For some the suffering they endure is a 'karmic condition', which means that it's a lesson to be learnt or a debt to be paid; the 'debt' may stem from a former existence. A 'karmic condition' may be cured if the spiritual development of the soul allows it. Every healing has a physical and a spiritual aspect.

Dr Robert is reluctant to speak about these things. It seems that, as long as we are on our present plane of consciousness, we are not supposed to get to the bottom of all the 'whys' and 'wherefores'. Apparently there's a limit to what Dr Robert is allowed to tell me about the ins

72

and outs of spiritual healing, and so I try to curb my curiosity. One thing is certain: every patient who comes to me benefits. Even if there's no cure, treatments impart a feeling of peace and harmony to the sufferer; there's always alleviation of pain and a stilling of anxieties.

Dr Robert once told me never to doubt; always to have hope, even for the very worst of cases.

'God's will be done,' he said. 'Stick to that and you'll never go wrong.'

Another lady belonging to my 'band of helpers' is Kay Norman, who came to my sanctuary in 1977 with serious eye trouble.

The sight of her right eye had begun to cloud over, and the specialist she consulted told her that the blood-vessels in that eye were breaking down, probably as a result of her blood pressure being too high. As soon as the affected blood-vessels started to recover, others would start breaking down.

She was in great distress, because she had a job in local government at that time and her eye trouble was beginning to interfere with her work. Her heart was also affected by the high blood pressure that had plagued her since 1969.

When she entered my sanctuary she could only see a red blur on the right eye, and the specialist's final verdict had been that there was no cure for her complaint and that she would go blind on that eye; also, there was always the fear that the same thing might happen to the other eye.

In her case the healing process took eighteen months, with visits at three monthly intervals. She was also on my absent healing list.

Today, at the age of sixty-five, both her eyes have perfect vision. The right eye, which had looked so bloodshot when she first came, is as bright and clear as can be; you would never guess that anything had been wrong with it.

She waited a year before confirming the cure – she wanted to be sure of its permanence. Then she wrote a charming letter confirming the healing.

'I was deeply aware of the healing power of Dr Robert flowing through your hands, bringing a calm and harmony which privileged me to know not only healing but also great spiritual upliftment . . .' she wrote. 'I have now informed my doctor that the bloodclots no longer form in my eye and that my vision has been clear for nearly a year. And yes – I told him why. To my astonishment he was not at all surprised!'

Kay Norman is herself psychic to a certain degree, though she has never been able to develop her gifts. Her work in local government, plus her housewifely duties, have taken up all her time. Now retired, she is still a very busy lady with many interests and a husband to look after; sometimes she helped me with the actual healing.

Dr Robert draws energy from me, his medium, during every healing session. I cannot explain the nature of this 'energy' nor the way in which it is tapped, but I can feel that some kind of vital essence is drawn from me. That's why I feel 'emptied' after a healing. The energy comes back quickly enough, but after a long day's sessions, when one patient after another has received healing. I can feel pretty exhausted.

The energy drawn from the medium can be 'boosted' by a helper, and this is what Kay Norman did for me. She used to place her hand on mine whilst I was treating a patient; part of the energy needed for the healing process could thus be drawn from her.

She did this service with great enthusiasm. 'I'm glad to be able to do something really useful in return for the marvellous healing I received,' she said.

Once, so she told me, when my hand was lying on the spine of a patient and she had covered my hand with hers, she could feel the patient's spine move: 'It was quite extraordinary; it was as if the spine had taken on a life of its own. I knew that it was Dr Robert at work and I felt quite proud at my being able to supply a little extra energy.'

Though today Kay is no longer my 'energy booster', she still comes along to help in many ways whenever she can spare the time, and Dr Robert continues to give her healing every now and then. He has managed to keep her heart trouble at bay and high blood pressure is no longer a problem.

'She's an easy patient,' he told me. 'Her positive thinking is of great help to the healing process.'

He was referring to her habit of using 'self-healing' thoughts; something he approves of totally.

There's also an artistic side to Kay Norman's nature. She writes short stories and poetry; more for her own pleasure than any other reason, but some of her poetry has been published, including a charming poem on spiritual healing; she dedicated it to me and called it *Pilgrimage of Healing*.

Our house at Patcham was by no means ideal. The fact that my patients had to climb stairs to reach the sanctuary caused great inconvenience, but the lay-out of the house was such that it was impossible to have it on the ground floor.

So, in 1973 we moved to the house in Hove, which proved to be damp. Something had to be done about it and we gladly accepted the Testers' invitation to stay with them.

All seemed well when we moved back, but Dr Robert wasn't happy with our new abode. He was trying to find the ideal place for us; ideal not only as a healing sanctuary, but also as a home for Phyllis and me.

'You don't think I'm going to let you stay here, do you,' he almost shouted one day. 'Oh no, we're going to move – and when I say "move", we move!' He was very excited and obviously had something up his sleeve.

Sure enough, not very much later we were guided to our present home, quite by chance. We saw this lovely two-storied house in a quiet district on the borders of Brighton and Hove. It lay in its own grounds, with a garden at the back and a garage; lots of space for a nice bright lounge and a sanctuary large enough to arrange and furnish exactly as I wished, and enough space upstairs to have a guest room. How nice it would be to invite friends to stay, we thought.

It was an expensive property and we really didn't think that we could afford it, but Dr Robert meant us to have it and so we got it in the end through the help of a good friend, a former patient, who later also helped with healing.

By 1975 we were installed in our lovely new home. I was very happy, especially for Phyllis, who not long ago had lost her only brother and she had been heartbroken. The new house helped to take her mind off her sorrow – there was so much to do.

We had also acquired a little toy poodle, whom we called 'Sparky'. He had come to us as a tiny pup, but by the time we moved into our new home he was fully grown. His new surroundings were very much to his liking and he tore through house and garden almost frantic with joy.

'Sparky' was very popular with the patients. He was part of the 'reception' and greeted each entrant with joyful barks and much tail-wagging.

Sadly, he left us in 1980, a very old dog by then, but bright and cheerful to the last. We miss him very much, and so do the patients who knew him.

One of the most distressing sights is surely that of a suffering child. My heart always goes out to the parents of a sick youngster, especially a baby.

For the small patients themselves I have a profound feeling of love and tenderness that wells up from the very depths of my being.

'Suffer little children to come unto me . . .' these words of Jesus, the great healer, echo in my mind whenever such a tiny one is brought to me. 'Who am I to carry on such a sacred tradition of healing?' I wonder. The thought humbles me. What a responsibility – to the parents, and to the little one himself!

76

Then I 'see' Dr Robert. He gazes at the child and its anxious parents. A whole world of love and compassion shines from his eyes. Now he looks up at me, smiles encouragingly and nods his head. I switch on the music and all thought is lost in our joint endeavour to bring healing to our little patient.

Early in 1975 Mr and Mrs Coppard came to me with their two-year-old son Stephen. The little boy's illness had defeated the most careful attempts at diagnosis and treatment. It had started when he was a tiny baby, with sudden bouts of fever, coughing, breathing difficulties and an inability to take his feeds. Doctors couldn't find anything organically wrong with him and thought he would 'grow out of it'.

He didn't; on the contrary, things got much worse. At about three months he started to have fits of screaming; not the normal yelling of a healthy, angry baby, but screams so vehement that they seemed to tear his little body apart. Throwing himself about in his cot, struggling for breath, his head would bang violently against the wooden bars. His terrified mother would pick him up, trying to soothe and comfort him and even then he would go on struggling and screaming.

His parents were at their wits end when a friend, rather vaguely, counselled them to try this 'so-called spirit healer', who, like themselves, lived in Brighton and would therefore be easy to contact. His name, said the friend, was Tom Pilgrim!

Unfortunately, when the Coppards rang to make an appointment, they didn't tell Phyllis how urgent their case was and were given a date three months hence. How I wish I could have saved them that long, anxious wait! I always manage to fit in emergencies at a shorter notice, particularly children; but in principle patients have to be seen on a strict rota, so as to be fair to all.

Anyway, the Coppards arrived with Stephen on the appointed day and were, I think, frankly dubious about the whole undertaking.

'He's been quiet today,' said Mrs Coppard shyly, 'but you never know when he'll start screaming again.'

I had picked up the little lad and held him in my arms. He looked at me out of large, astonished eyes. With his mother's permission I offered him a sweet. Solemnly he reached for it, popped it in his mouth and gave me a radiant smile.

Dr Robert was already there, watching and waiting.

Stephen, solemn again, sat very quietly after I had placed him on the patients' stool. I asked him if he liked music. He nodded, and when the tape was running – I had selected a very soothing, melodious theme – he closed his eyes and seemed to listen with rapt attention.

I saw Dr Robert nod his head: his signal to begin the healing.

Although I no longer go into trance when I have music to anchor my consciousness, I'm nevertheless very strongly overshadowed by Dr Robert as he takes over and the power pours through me. Some healing sessions take more out of me than others; this one had me perspiring, and I was trembling when Dr Robert withdrew, giving me to understand that Stephen was going to be cured. I felt exhausted and very happy.

The parents, watching attentively, told me they were amazed at the way Stephen had sat there, quietly listening to the music; not moving at all whilst Dr Robert was guiding my hands to his head, his chest, his tummy and then back to his head.

'There was no wheezing at all!' exclaimed the astonished father. 'His breath seemed to come quite easily all the time. That's most unusual.'

'He'll be alright now,' I said. 'He's fine – you'll see. I'd like you to bring him again once or twice, my wife will fix the appointments. You no longer have to worry, your son is cured.'

As I picked Stephen up and placed him in his mother's arms I knew that he was healed. The process only had to complete itself.

The Coppards later confessed that as they left the sanctuary they had still been doubtful. It had all been so inexplicable: two years of pain and discomfort for their son; anxiety, fear, sleepless nights and despair for them;

after so much fruitless medical treatment, how could Stephen be cured almost within minutes? They then related how their doubts had been shaken that same night when Stephen, suddenly violently sick, had looked better the moment he had stopped vomiting and had then slept soundly throughout the night without waking once.

'We really felt hopeful the next morning,' said Mrs Coppard. 'We knew that something tremendously good had happened to Stephen.'

The little boy improved steadily and after the last of his treatments he was playing about out of doors and eating and sleeping normally. He had become a happy, healthy child and has remained so, as his mother confirmed three trouble-free years later.

Many healers find that there are certain complaints which respond particularly well to their method of healing.

Over the years I have found that eye trouble, arthritis, rheumatism and all manner of spinal complaints respond most readily to Dr Robert's treatments, and once again I cannot explain why this should be so. It has certainly nothing to do with the type of work Dr Robert specialised in when on earth; as I've said before, the 'whys' and 'wherefores' often elude me.

Our eyesight being one of the most precious faculties given to us, anything that threatens to impair or destroy it, causes deep anxiety and distress.

The eye being such a delicate organ, healing has to proceed gently and may take time; yet, in some cases, a single treatment can have quite spectacular results.

I have before me a letter written on November 6 in 1976, by Mrs Iva Cosgrove of Hove, who reports as follows: 'I am writing to say how very grateful I am to you, and your wonderful helpers in the spirit world, for the amazing healing I had from you last Tuesday, November 2nd.

'Having had a completely blind eye for the past two years, I can now see nearly as well with it as with my right, good eye.

'I can even see colour, and each day it is becoming clearer. I am so thrilled and happy to be able to tell you this . . .'

One of the most poignant cases I have come across as far as eye-troubles are concerned, was that of Andrew Keeley. His trouble had started in 1976 with an irritation in his left eye; nothing much at first, just a slight discomfort at times, with watering and occasional redness. It got worse and he went to his doctor, who diagnosed conjunctivitis. This, however, was a wrong diagnosis. Hospital examination revealed that he had diabetes, which had caused haemorrhages behind the eye. He was put on a strict diet and had to attend the hospital's out-patients department for special treatment. There was no improvement of the eye condition, on the contrary, vision of the affected eye began to deteriorate.

By August 1977 the left eye had become sightless. The specialist at the hospital stopped bothering about it and concentrated on saving the right eye, which had started to show the same symptoms.

When Andrew Keeley told me all this he was at the end of his tether. Not only was his whole life's work in jeopardy, he had planned to get married in the near future.

'Saddle my Mary with a near blind and eventually a completely blind husband? Never!' he exclaimed.

'Who talks here of blindness?' I queried.

'Well, that's what I'm heading for, isn't it?'

Quite clearly, he had no faith whatsoever; yet, fate had given him a pointer which should have indicated to him that there is a power that guides and directs our lives.

He had met his future wife, a widow, three years previously – long before his eye trouble had started. Mary knew about spirit healing, because her first husband had once, years ago, been a patient of Mr Tester. Now, in her despair over Keeley's condition, she had remembered Tester and had contacted him and he, knowing that I had been successful with eye-complaints, had referred her to me.

'I've no faith, you know,' he said with a wry smile.

'Never mind that, I've enough faith for both of us,' I answered.

I knew that all would be well, for there stood Dr Robert, ready and eager to start the treatment.

'He'll be alright,' I heard him say quite clearly and I've never known Dr Robert to be wrong.

When the first session was over, my 'doubting Thomas' of a patient told me how the moment the music had started and he had felt my hands on him, a soothing, relaxing wave of comfort and ease had swept over him; the terrible tension that had held him as in a vice for months had dissolved like mist when the sun breaks through. Harmony, peace, and with that a bright ray of hope had entered his consciousness.

He rose from the stool a different human being.

Mary, who had been sitting close by during the healing, looked at me questioningly.

'The healing process has started,' I said. 'When it's completed his vision will be as bright and clear as that of any healthy pair of eyes.'

We arranged an 'absent healing' time, each night at 10.30, and fixed the next apointment.

Very much later Andrew Keeley confessed: 'You know, Mr Pilgrim, I knew after that first session that I would be cured. My doubts had simply vanished!'

The first time he went back to the hospital for a routine examination, the specialist was amazed to find that his patient could see a little in the left eye – the one that had gone completely blind.

Improvement continued, and when Andrew married his Mary in April 1978, his sight was completely restored.

'That was our most wonderful wedding present,' he commented in an interview for the Spiritualist weekly paper *Psychic News*.

In June 1977 the TV actor Bill Maynard came to see me. He was in agony over a 'slipped disc'. It had become so bad that the only part he was able to play at the time was that of an invalid in a wheelchair. Doctors had given him a steel-lined corset, which they told him he must wear at all times.

I had often seen Bill Maynard on television and had enjoyed his performances and his particular brand of humour very much indeed. It made my heart ache to see him in such pain and I could well imagine his fear of becoming a helpless cripple, no longer able to work in the profession he loved so much.

Dr Robert excelled himself. 'We'll have him right in no time,' he said.

The man who had lowered himself slowly and painfully onto my stool relaxed visibly as I switched on the music and came over to him. Dr Robert's guiding hands went straight to the seat of pain on Maynard's spine. I felt the power flowing through me, felt the spine move, felt my hands being moved up and down Maynard's back. Then, suddenly, it was done. Dr Robert moved away from me; 'that's it,' he said, smiling broadly. 'He's cured – tell him to get rid of that damned corset!'

I switched off the tape and turned to look at my patient. There he sat, wearing an expression of blank surprise.

'The pain's gone!'

'Yes, and it won't come back either,' I said. 'Get up, you're cured.'

'You mean it's all over? In one short session?' He just couldn't believe it.

'The proof of the pudding is in the eating,' I answered. 'Just get up!'

He did, and exclaimed again: 'No pain, no pain at all!'

When he was up I placed a book at his feet. 'Pick it up,' I said.

Before the healing he could not have bent down to save his life. He picked up the book without difficulty, held it high and said over and over again, 'Marvellous – simply marvellous . . .'

'What's more,' I said, 'you can take that corset off – it's no longer needed.'

He did so, then and there; Phyllis wrapped it up in brown paper and the delighted actor threw the parcel into the sea.

Bill Maynard gave his story to the *Sunday Mirror*,

which gave a fair account of the healing. 'Spirit beings' always seem to bother the press; still, the report did mention 'the spirit of a German surgeon'.

I heard Dr Robert chuckle as I read the article.

The 'Maynard story' made Miss Rachel Collins, a lady in her seventies, suffering from back trouble and arthritis, think: 'Why not give it a try? Perhaps he'll be able to cure my back – as he did the actor's.'

Her troubles had started when she was but fifteen years old with a rheumatic bone condition. Gradually, the condition had spread, and by the time she was thirty she was 'but a bag of pains and aches', as she herself put it.

'My hands became more and more crippled; it was horrible. I had every treatment for arthritis known to medical science: beestings, gold injections, drugs – the lot! Nothing seemed to make the slightest difference.

'Going to hospital, during one period three times a week, was sheer hell; a hiatus hernia added to my misery and I had two operations. Then I had angina, and at sixty-four a "slipped disc" after which I was popped into a steel corset and given two sticks. The corset restricted my already limited movements and I fell and broke my elbow!'

This tale of woe only emerged later, after she had been healed. To start with she told me only about the 'awful pain in the back'; she didn't mention anything else, because she had been convinced that her arthritis was incurable. They had told her so at the hospital. Of course I could see with my own eyes what the main trouble was. The unmistakable symptoms of arthritis showed themselves only too clearly; but there was Dr Robert, giving me a detailed diagnosis of every one of Rachel Collins' ills since childhood. 'Ask her to take the corset off straight away,' he concluded.

She complied, and then, with my help, lowered herself onto the stool. She was in great pain. I could see her fingers clutching the handles at the side of the stool, the knuckles turning white as she tightened her grip.

'Try to relax. Close your eyes, forget everything that bothers you and think of something pleasant.'

As I came over to her after I had switched on the tape and the music was playing, the tension in her tortured body slowly eased up, and when my hands lay upon her back and my consciousness became overshadowed by that of Dr Robert, she relaxed completely.

'I felt heat streaming from your hands,' she told me afterwards. 'It was a wonderful, soothing feeling. Then there was a vibration that seemed to go right through me!'

She just sat there, not daring to move, after I'd switched off the music. I knew from Dr Robert that the arthritis as well as the slipped disc had been cured.

'You can get up now,' I said.

She made a move towards her corset and her sticks.

'No, no!' I laid a restraining hand on her arm. 'You won't need them. You'll never want them again – ever,' I said with the emphasis on the last word.

Rachel Collins got to her feet, a look of amazement on her face. 'You're right, I can move and nothing hurts anywhere,' she exclaimed.

I asked her to bend down; something she hadn't been able to do in years. She did it without the slightest trouble.

'Heavens!' she moved her limbs, stretching and bending arms and legs.

'I can move the lot without feeling even a twinge!'

It was sheer joy to see this lady walk out of my sanctuary – tears of happiness in her eyes – carrying her walking sticks before her like trophies, and having stuffed 'the nasty corset' into her handbag.

'Next day I walked to the chemist,' she told Phyllis and me later. 'You should have seen their faces when I marched in without sticks and plonked all my drugs on the counter with the words: "I no longer need them, thank you very much!"'

She comes for treatment every three months now, which keeps her angina at bay. Her back trouble and arthritis, cured in that one session in 1977, never returned. Today an immensely lively, active lady of seventy-six, she has become a very dear friend of Phyllis and myself.

In many cases it is not only a sick body, but also a sick mind that needs healing. Sometimes the physical suffering is so intense, that the patient gives way to hopelessness and resignation. It needs great inner strength to combat a feeling of 'oh, what's the use?' when again and again hopes of a cure or even alleviation of pain are dashed; should that strength waver and break down, a patient may sink into a grey trough of despair from which he cannot rise. Drugs, taken to dull the pain, also dull the functions of the brain and the patient's willpower sinks to an even lower ebb. Caught in a vicious circle of body and mind acting and reacting upon each other, the sufferer simply gives up.

Such a patient was Ivan Brown, of Southwick, Sussex. A giant of a man, six feet tall, who had been a keen sportsman, a loving husband and father, who had romped and played with his son until, after a fall in 1966, his back had started to give him trouble.

At the hospital nothing could be found wrong with it; but the pain, bearable at first, had been getting steadily worse and had started to affect his legs as well. He was a self-employed painter and decorator who loved his trade, but the work, once a pleasure, became a daily, agonising struggle. A second fall, though not at all serious, seemed to make things worse. He kept on visiting the hospital, but to no avail, and by the time his twin daughters Mary and Julie were born in 1970, he was almost an invalid. Eight years later, at the age of thirty-eight, he had become a helpless cripple. He could no longer work. Climbing the stairs up to the bedroom at home meant agony over every step negotiated. Lack of exercise had made his huge frame put on excessive weight, which made moving even more painful and laborious. Diet brought the weight down again, but doctors didn't really know what to do with this man: no diagnosis could be made of what it was that caused the excruciating pains he was suffering. None of the known treatments, such as physiotherapy, traction, manipulation, had brought him any relief.

In the end he was sleeping on the floor at home – downstairs, of course – and at the hospital, where they had fitted him with the mandatory steel corset, they had dismissed him with the old cliché: 'You'll have to learn to live with it.'

The man who entered my sanctuary on May 2, 1978, looked and moved like a zombie. Physically, mentally and spiritually defeated, he had only come to me because his wife had begged him to do so. There was no light in his eyes; his voice was devoid of tone, his speech halting and monotonous. He stood on the sanctuary threshold like an immovable object, rooted to the ground. When I came forward to greet him he took my outstretched hand, but made no move to enter the room.

'Come, sit down and relax,' I said, taking his arm and guiding him gently to the stool.

I could see Dr Robert standing there, watching us, and silently conveyed to him my deep concern over this patient, who, in his utter hopelessness, seemed beyond reach, encapsulated in his prison of pain.

Dr Robert responded with a nod, indicating that he was ready to begin the healing. His expression told me that he, too, was concerned; but he gave me to understand that it was Ivan's state of mind that worried him far more than his physical disability.

I asked the patient to remove his corset. He did it with the utmost reluctance and only after I had assured him that he would suffer no ill effects from doing so. There he sat – like a great, big lump of dough, expecting nothing but pain.

During the healing I became conscious of Dr Robert concentrating on one particular spot on the patient's spine. I felt my fingertips digging in hard and pushing at something – once, twice. Then I heard Dr Robert say 'That's it! That's it!'

My shirt was wet with perspiration when it was all over. I felt utterly exhausted. Switching off the tape and wiping my forehead, I could hear Dr Robert explain that two of the little cushions that sit between the discs of a spine had become dislodged. It would not show on an X-ray. He had pushed the cushions back into place. 'He's cured – we'll have to watch the state of his mind, that's all,' he concluded.

It took some persuasion to make Ivan even stand up, and when I placed a block of wood at his feet, asking him to pick it up, he looked at me as if to say, 'Have you gone mad?'

'Look, you could rise from that stool without pain or effort, couldn't you?' I asked him.

'Yes, but ...'

'You can do it! Bend down and pick up that wood,' I said firmly.

He did so – hesitatingly at first, but when he found there was no pain at all, he reached right down to his feet, took the block in his hands, straightened up again and stood there, with an expression of, 'I don't understand' on his face.

I put an arm round his shoulder and explained gently that he was cured; that there would be no more pain; no more visits to hospitals and specialists. 'You'll be able to live life and enjoy it like any other healthy human being. Your wife is waiting for you in the car, outside, isn't she?'

'Yes.'

'Well, go and tell her the good news!'

It took a long time before Ivan's crushed spirit revived. Twelve years of pain and hopeless quests for a cure brought to an end in a few minutes? For some patients such a realisation comes with a rush of joy, tears and emotion and a feeling of instant, blessed relief.

For one who had sunk into such terrible depths of despair the final healing of mind and spirit could only come slowly; but it came, and today Ivan Brown is back at work, a happy family man, and once again able to enjoy a game of football.

His gratitude was touching. I cut him short when he was trying to thank me and explained that I was just a channel for God's healing power – besides, I had a helper, I told him.

He accepted Dr Robert. 'Yes, I believe you,' he said. 'Thank him for me, please! I feel a miracle has happened to me – he's given me back my life – I can never thank him enough!'

Chapter 7

Home and Abroad

There is no short cut to true achievement. That goes for all who work in a spiritual realm as well as for anyone else. Whether we're mediums or healers or both, our psychic gifts must be developed and used in the right way before success is granted us.

My 'testing time' had ended with the vision of the cross and Dr Robert Koch's appearance. From that time onwards I knew what I had to do; but it was only the first step on a long road that was by no means strewn with roses. I received many a setback, even from quarters I had looked to for help. During one particularly unhappy period, when certain promises made to me were not kept, I worked without stopping for no reward and in the end fell ill with bronchitis.

Just as my mother had foretold, I suffered 'disappointments, scorn and disbelief,' but gradually acknowledgement and recognition came – and in any case, the sight of a baby healed, a patient saved from blindness, crippled limbs made straight, or tears of emotion in the eyes of someone who had given up and against all odds had received a new lease of life, made it all worthwhile.

Today patients come to my sanctuary in Brighton from all over the world. Sometimes, at weekends, people from the Continent – mostly Austria or Switzerland – drive out to me straight from Heathrow and after healing straight back to Heathrow to catch a plane home.

To cope with the growing demand for healing, Phyllis and I have evolved a strict routine: Tuesdays and Wednesdays I heal at my sanctuary, Fridays I visit hospitals or people's homes; Thursdays are reserved for answering letters – never less than one hundred – and on weekends there may be a public demonstration in Brighton or elsewhere. On an average I see about fifteen patients a day. Mondays I try to rest.

Demands for hospital visits are increasing. The BMA (British Medical Association) recognised spiritual healers officially in 1979 and since then doctors often refer patients to healers and even consult them for their own ailments. Some had cooperated with healers long before official recognition, but as it had been frowned upon by medical orthodoxy, they had to keep it quiet.

Nowadays my visits to hospitals are made with the permission of doctors and staff, and I'm always received with the utmost courtesy.

My 'bedside manner' is a very silent one, because I have to ask the patient not to talk whilst I'm healing; very important in hospital, where I have no music to keep my consciousness 'anchored'. I go into trance the moment Dr Robert takes over. After so many years of experience I can prevent a very deep trance, but it's not so easy and it helps if patients just relax and do not break the concentration by talking.

At public demonstrations I do have music; I also have Phyllis by my side, and sometimes, to ours and Dr Robert's great joy, an instantaneous cure happens in full view of the audience.

During one Brighton demonstration a man suffering from arthritis had a completely locked arm freed. Michael Endicott, at that time administrator of the National Federation of Spiritual Healers, was on the platform when it happened. He commented on the way the patient's fingers began to move and how the arm gradually loosened and, after years of rigidity, could once again be moved freely.

Dorothy Dragon, a lady with a painful stomach ulcer, wrote to confirm a complete cure after receiving a 'spirit operation' during a demonstration at the Brighton Technical College in 1981.

'I was in great pain at the time, but felt no pain during the operation,' she writes; 'it was a most wonderful experience as I watched you working on me. The operation was a complete success.'

I became a member of the 'National Federation of Spiritual Healers' in 1973 – their certificate is displayed in my office. It is an organisation that vets healers, making sure they are genuine, as well as defending and sometimes fighting for healers' rights. Official recognition of spiritual healing by the BMA is largely due to the Healers Federation's efforts, and now there's a movement afoot to make spiritual healing available under the National Health Service.

Few healers charge fees. Most of us consider our healing ability to be a gift of God, to be given freely to all who need it; but even a healer has to live, and so we accept donations. A part of what I receive goes to charity.

Patients can be very generous – but not all of them approach healing in a spirit of humility and gratitude. One rather abrasive elderly lady said to me after she had been cured: 'I'm not giving you a donation. After all, God gave you your gift!'

To which I could only reply: 'Yes, Madam, God gave me my gift, but he also gave me my stomach ...'

Dr Robert will accept any patient – he is only too willing to help, to heal, to lessen the sufferings of mankind; but he is also a man who doesn't suffer fools gladly. He told me so, and he also told me that we do not change our basic character when we leave earth life for the next stage of being. A fact I had already learnt from the example of my mother and father, who had remained essentially the same, retaining the characteristics I had known and loved.

With all the selfless service Dr Robert gives to humanity, he still retains his basic traits; like any other human being in this world or the next, he can feel happy or sad, elated, frustrated or hurt; he can get impatient, excited, angry and – rarely – very cross indeed.

He once got me into a highly embarrassing situation: an elderly spinster, suffering from arthritis, arrived for her second healing session in an aggressive mood: 'I'm no better than when I came to you last time,' she shouted on entering the sanctuary. Brushing me aside, she went up to Dr Robert's picture, wagging her finger at him: 'And it's about time you did something as well,' she stormed.

Dr Robert, who stood near the door with eyebrows raised and arms folded across his chest, took one look at the lady as she stood finger-wagging before his portrait, gave a snort of disgust, turned on his heels and left the sanctuary.

There I stood – with no spirit doctor and a waiting room full of patients. Annoyed with the lady's behaviour and desperately worried about what was going to happen if Dr Robert didn't return, I said to her: 'I'm very sorry, Madam, but I don't think I can help you,' whereupon she marched out in a huff.

When the next patient entered, Dr Robert was back again. He still looked angry, but as he approached the humble, patient looking man who had seated himself on the stool, he gave me a reassuring smile.

'You didn't think I'd leave you?' he said.

Like any doctor on earth, Dr Robert can call on helpers, or 'second opinions', if he wants to. Richard Gouldon, a famous eye-surgeon who used to work at the Royal Free Hospital, London, during his earth life, assists with eye complaints, and there's another German physician, Dr Heinemann, whom Dr Robert sometimes calls in, and a Chinese doctor, known to me simply as 'Chang'.

An interesting feature is the so-called 'guardian of the door'. Every healer and every medium has one. He (it can, of course, also be a 'she') is a kind of spirit 'doorkeeper' who guards against the intrusion of unwanted spirit entities into the medium's or healer's aura. Mine is an African, called Zambula. He takes no part in the healing, but is an important member of Dr Robert's group. His function is a very necessary one, as unpleasant and even dangerous beings inhabit the world of spirit just as they inhabit ours.

I have, on occasions, seen all the members of Dr Robert's group gathered around a patient, but Dr Robert is the leader; it is 'his' group and those who work with him have accepted this. They never appear unbidden, but come whenever Dr Robert needs their opinions and advice.

Sometimes they surround a hospital bed when I'm treating an 'in' patient, and they most certainly help with 'absent healing'.

Among patients cured in hospital was a seven-week-old baby that had been born in 1979 with only one kidney – and a diseased one at that. Doctors at Guy's Hospital, London, held out no hope for little Ian's survival and had informed his parents of the hopelessness of his case.

It was Ian's grandfather, Erick Franklin, who asked me if I could help; the baby's parents knew nothing of his request and would probably have taken a dim view of it if they had known. They were complete disbelievers when it came to psychic matters. This meant that I couldn't go to the hospital to treat the baby, and the cure was achieved entirely by absent healing.

For a fortnight I concentrated on Ian twice daily at the same time, and the miracle happened: the baby was allowed home, with his diseased kidney cured.

'Forget that your son has only one kidney; he's a fine, healthy baby now,' doctors told the delighted parents.

The grandfather never let on 'who' or 'what' cured his grandson. Ian's parents still share the doctors' belief that a wrong diagnosis had been made; though the medics – as Mr Franklin told me later – were more than puzzled by the whole case. There had been absolutely no doubt that the baby had been practically at death's door and they couldn't understand what had brought about the sudden change in his condition.

Baby Ian's case proves that psychic healing has nothing to do with 'faith', 'suggestion' or 'imagination', and is also a wonderful example of the efficacy of 'absent healing'.

I'm always particularly happy when a child has been cured, and I remember how pleased Dr Robert and I were when a little girl's eyesight was saved in 1979.

Eleven-year-old Anita Southon, from Southampton, had undergone two eye operations when she was hardly more than a toddler. Her eye-muscles were very weak and she could not focus properly. She had great difficulty at school and each time her eyes were tested the optician prescribed stronger glasses.

Anita's parents brought her to me after they had read a report about my work in *Psychic News*. She had five healing-sessions, her sight improving with each one. After the fifth her father told me that the breakthrough had come: 'We were playing a ball game and Anita managed to catch the ball; something she hadn't been able to do before. Her grandfather challenged her to take her glasses off and try again, and to our amazement she caught the ball quite easily – without her glasses!'

Anita's eyes are fine now – when her mother can't thread a needle, she does it for her.

How I sympathised with John Hickey, a Brighton patient who came to see me – also in 1979 – after an ear, nose and throat specialist had told him he needed an operation which entailed having his nose broken! Remembering my own horror at being threatened with an operation involving the breaking of my jaw, I promised to do my very best for him.

John Hickey is a Spiritualist, so it was easy to tell him about Dr Robert, and he responded with telling me the story of how he had come to seek my help: 'I've been plagued by sinusitis for years, and finally it got so bad that I had to consult an ear, nose and throat specialist; after examining me he said I had a twisted septum (partition) in my nose and needed an operation. This would mean breaking my nose, straightening the septum or replacing it by a plastic one, and then a skin graft – in other words a new nose!

'You can imagine my dismay at this prospect! Well, I had a wonderful sitting with Jim Hutchings, the Brighton medium, during which his spirit guide counselled me not to submit to the operation, but to seek the help of a spiritual healer. Jim Hutchings later gave me your name and telephone number.'

When Hickey phoned me I was booked up for months ahead at my Brighton sanctuary but I could offer him an appointment in London, where I was giving treatments the following week. Absurd, really – seeing that we both live in Brighton; but Mr Hickey didn't mind.

'I'd go anywhere to get healing,' he said.

Later he told me that on the day he had travelled to London he had felt particularly bad.

'I had such a blinding headache that even walking seemed to make it worse. However, as soon as I entered the room where you were working, I felt a sense of well-being. Then, at one point during the healing – you had placed your hands on my nose – it felt as if a heavy weight was being lifted out of the top of my head, and in that instant the headache disappeared.'

Dr Robert, performing a 'spirit operation', had straightened the septum.

'I felt better than I had done for years as I walked back to Victoria Station to catch my train home,' John Hickey continued.

'I dozed off in the train, happy to have been relieved of my headache; I woke to see a man bending over me, seemingly examining my nose. Funny way that man's dressed, I thought muzzily, not quite awake yet – then, in a flash, I realised that this man in old-fashioned clothes was none other than Dr Robert!'

He was quite right. Dr Robert confirmed that he had taken a quick look at his patient asleep in the train, 'just to check that all was in order,' he said. 'He woke just as I was bending over him and caught a glimpse of me.'

In the moment between sleeping and waking it can happen that people who are not normally clairvoyant or clairaudient catch climpses of spirit beings or hear a spirit being's voice.

Dr Robert is usually careful not to show himself to patients if he can help it. One woman patient who saw him one night during her 'absent healing' time screamed in terror. He was very indignant at what he considered her 'illogical reaction'.

'What was she afraid of?' he queried. 'Seeing me should have been a confirmation that I really do exist; comforting, one would have throught, in view of the fact that I'm supposed to be healing her!'

John Hickey was delighted at his catching sight of Dr Robert: 'There he was – so real, so solid! And it was certainly not my imagination, nor was it a fleeting impression, but something that lasted a good thirty to forty-five seconds.'

Some time later, when Hickey was on holiday in Germany, he happened to meet an ear, nose and throat specialist and asked him if he would have a look at his nose, telling him he was supposed to have a 'twisted septum'. The specialist checked and found the septum perfectly straight.

John Hickey's cure – achieved in a single sitting – meant a great improvement in his social as well as in his professional life. Public speaking, for instance, which he has to do quite frequently at Spiritualist meetings or services, used to cause him great problems because of the nasal congestion he used to suffer. Now he enjoys every opportunity to speak and has more than once told audiences the story of his 'spirit operation'.

Interest in 'spiritual' or 'psychic' healing has become world wide and for quite a number of years now reputable British healers have been travelling abroad, giving public and private demonstrations.

Laws governing healing practices vary from country to country and British healers have to be careful not to offend against the laws of the country they are visiting.

In August 1977 I was invited, together with Phyllis, by

a Spiritualist group in Switzerland to come over and give healing demonstrations to a private circle of invited guests. This was quite permissible under the Swiss legal system and I was glad to accept.

Zurich, seat of the 'International Spiritualist Federation', was our first port of call. Our hosts had arranged for my healing sessions to take place in their home and had invited patients. I was overwhelmed by the warmth of our reception and the gratitude of the patients I treated.

It was only a short visit – a week in Zurich and another in Lugano. Both are beautiful cities and in Lugano we also had something of a holiday, with time to relax and enjoy the beautiful scenery. Altogether a pleasant and successful venture, which we repeated the following year.

Then, in 1979, we set out on the first of our 'great Canadian adventures'. We had been asked to undertake a six-week tour of Canada, giving public healing demonstrations in several cities.

We were sponsored by Mr Hubert Gray, a wealthy Canadian businessman, who had been my patient, been cured of rheumatism and had subsequently become a good friend of ours.

Hubert Gray also suffers from diabetes, which up to now has not been cured. Certain diseases are more resistant to healing than others, diabetes and cancer being two of the most difficult to cure, but, as the case of leukaemia cured by Dr Robert more than thirty years ago proves, spiritual healing had succeeded in isolated cases to heal patients even of these complaints.

Dr Robert told me that physicians on his side of life are working just as hard on the solution of such problems as doctors here on earth. Mr Gray had accepted this and, encouraged by his being healed of a painful rheumatic condition, had worked out the itinerary for a Canadian tour.

A rumour had been put about in Canada that 'a British healer had conned Canadians'.

'We'll show them that spiritual healing is no "con" but

a fact, and I'll bring them the best British healer I know to prove it,' said Hubert Gray.

The tour was arranged down to the last detail, and apart from receiving the most lavish hospitality and being treated as VIPs wherever we went, we found an immense interest in psychic healing among Canadians of every walk of life.

I gave public healing demonstrations in Calgary, Vancouver and Victoria; three in each of these towns and on every occasion the halls were packed beyond capacity, with people standing in the gangways.

I remember a lady with an arm locked rigid from an attack of polio. It was freed then and there, at one of the demonstrations in Victoria; and a doctor at another demonstration, whose hearing was restored on the spot. His right ear had been completely deaf.

Private healings I gave in patients' homes, except that during our stay in Victoria I worked mostly in the home of Pat McCullogh, a friend of ours. Her dining-room had been turned into a makeshift 'sanctuary' and 'office' for me.

The aftermath of each public demonstration was a continuously ringing telephone. Morning, noon and night people rang to ask for appointments and it was quite impossible to accommodate more than a fraction of all the callers. I took as many as I could and must have seen at least one hundred people privately. Later I was told I had achieved a success rate of roughly eighty per cent. Dr Robert was delighted!

Among my private patients was a young woman, Cheryl Kuntz, who confirmed her cure when Phyllis and I were already back in London. She had been badly hurt in a car accident and came to me in despair because one of her knees, injured in the crash, would not mend. She could hardly bend it and it gave her constant pain. She came to me twice – at the time of the first session her knee would not bend by more than thirty-five degrees.

'You'll be able to bend your knee properly again,' I said. Dr Robert had just told me so, and after the second session, when they checked the knee again at the hospital, it had a bend of thirty-seven degrees.

I had also placed her on my absent healing list, and in February 1980 she reported in a letter of acknowledgement published in *The Seeker* (news letter of the Chrysalis Development Society, Canada): 'Now I have a bend of eighty-six degrees in that knee! I thank Tom Pilgrim for what he did for me.'

Valerie Saunders of Victoria had suffered from a degenerate disc disease in the lower back for the best part of eight years. When she came to me it had become so bad that she could neither sit nor walk because of the excruciating pain it caused her. Doctors had told her there was nothing they could do: 'Take it easy,' was their advice.

She was a little disappointed when she didn't receive an instant 'miracle cure', as she put it. I explained that it wasn't always possible to achieve immediate relief and asked her to follow her doctor's advice and 'take it easy' for the next forty-eight hours. Dr Robert would come and visit her early next morning to check on the result of the 'spirit operation' he had performed and to make sure that she was making satisfactory progress.

As a keen student of spiritual and psychic matters she accepted all I told her about Dr Robert Koch and his continued service to mankind.

'I went to sleep that night secure in the knowledge that I had been healed and that time would lessen the pain, much as after an ordinary physical operation,' she reported later.

After a week the pain ceased completely. No more nagging backache at the end of a day and to her immense joy she could even ride her horse again without the slightest discomfort.

'But the real shock came about a month later,' she wrote at the end of her report. 'I was scratching my back and my hand passed over my spine just where the three deteriorating vertebrae had been sticking out . . . and they weren't sticking out anymore! The diseased vertebrae had moved into place with the rest of my back and, once again, I had a strong, healthy spine.

'There is no doubt in my mind that I received the "miracle cure" I had been seeking.'

The 1979 tour had been so successful that Phyllis and I were invited to return to Canada the following year for two months. So, off we went again in the summer of 1980, visiting the same towns.

Our first public demonstration at the Queen Victoria Inn, Victoria, was such an overwhelming success, that a second session had to be held on public demand.

One incident that caused a sensation was the instant cure of a man whose foot was set rigid through arthritis. He couldn't walk, only hobble about painfully with the aid of sticks.

After ten minutes healing he walked the length of the hall: 'Look, Tom, look at my foot,' he cried; 'I can walk!'

I appeared on the Joe Easingwood radio programme, broadcast from Victoria, which resulted in a flood of telephone calls from people wanting appointments. Once again I could only see a small percentage of all the people clamouring for healing and it saddened me to have to refuse help to so many, but Dr Robert was adamant and insisted on keeping the number of patients down to what I could manage without overstraining myself.

'It wouldn't be much help if you collapsed and I had to start healing *you* – now would it!' he chided when I tried to exceed the number of patients he thought reasonable.

He was right, of course. Demonstration tours are very strenuous, especially abroad. You are away from your accustomed environment and routine, climate and food are different and the whole tempo of life is speeded up. You see many more patients than you would at home and public demonstrations bring an added nervous strain; then come the press interviews, publicity arrangements, invitations and entertainments, none of which you can refuse, because they are part and parcel of the commitments you agreed to accept. Besides, who could be so churlish as to refuse invitations extended with such warmth and enthusiasm as was shown to us – however tired one may feel!

It is, in any case, a fantastic experience and I'm more than grateful to Hubert Gray for having given us such marvellous opportunities to demonstrate psychic healing in his country.

We met many interesting people and sometimes a social occasion would provide a special opportunity to heal. I remember one such case very vividly, because it resulted in a remarkable cure.

During our stay at Calgary we were invited by Duncan Crockford, a famous Canadian painter and his wife, who lived miles out of town. It was a trip through lovely countryside which we enjoyed very much.

Our hosts were charming. We had tea, chatted, walked round the garden and Phyllis and I greatly appreciated the calm, relaxed atmosphere. After some time another guest arrived: a pleasant young man in his early thirties. At one point our host took me aside and asked if I would be so kind and give the young man healing.

'Gladly,' I said. 'What's wrong with him?'

'He's been in a very bad car crash; his kneecap was practically torn off. It was put back by surgery but later arthritis set in and it's become very painful indeed. You see, he's one of Calgary Hospital's top surgeons and often has to stand for hours when he's operating. The pain in his knee is so intense at times that he can hardly perform his duties.'

I gave the young man healing and told him to rest a while; then I went to the top of the house, where our host had a small exhibition of paintings. I received one as a gift, in fact, and whilst we were all upstairs, admiring the pictures, the young man suddenly came bounding up the stairs, calling out to us: 'Tom's healed my knee! Look, look how I can run upstairs! I could never have done this before the healing he gave me – there's no pain in that knee, none at all – it's fabulous!'

He wrote to me later, when we were back in England,

and his story appeared in *Psychic News*.

'This cure is a milestone in my life – I shall never forget it,' he reported.

I'm not at liberty to mention his name. He begged me not to give it; it could harm his reputation at the hospital. It is not for me to question his decision; perhaps the medical profession in Canada has not yet arrived at a point where spiritual healing can be officially recognised and where, as in Britain, physicians and spiritual healers can cooperate.

Dr Robert was disappointed: 'Acknowledgement of healing by some person well-known in his profession – especially if he is a medical man – can do much to dissipate prejudice and to encourage greater tolerance and a more open-minded public attitude.'

Mrs Learoyd in Victoria asked for healing for her grandson, Mark. He had a chest condition that wouldn't yield to any treatment. It had started when he was about eleven months old with coughing and wheezing. The usual remedies didn't work and the condition got steadily worse. Doctors diagnosed chronic bronchitis.

His parents took him to Hawaii, hoping the warm climate there and lots of sunshine would cure him, but it didn't seem to have the desired effect.

When I arrived at Victoria his grandmother arranged an appointment and little Mark was brought to me, more or less as a 'last resort'. He was a toddler by now, pale and very thin.

Once again Dr Robert excelled himself – Mark was cured in a single healing session. Today he's a sturdy, jolly little fellow with never a hint of his former trouble.

Telephone calls and letters asking for 'absent healing' still reach me here in Britain as a result of our first two Canadian trips, and in 1981 we went again – but that's another story.

In the meantime, back in Brighton, an ever mounting number of patients arrived at my doorstep.

'Does it never get you down?' asked a friend. Well, yes,

there are times when I feel overwhelmed by the sufferings I witness day by day, and sometimes I ask myself what's wrong with mankind that it should be burdened with so many ills; but I never get tired of healing, of transmitting God's love and compassion to all who come to me seeking help, and I feel a great sense of responsibility towards Dr Robert, who chose me as his instrument, and to all the selfless helpers in the spirit world. We can never fully appreciate the sacrifice these spirit beings make in staying close to our sphere in order to help us, when they could by rights move on to higher and infinitely more beautiful regions.

To me, a cure achieved, a soul opened up to the reality of spirit life are reward enough. Weariness and occasional feelings of distress are more than compensated by a patient healed. I cannot think of any other work that could bring such 'job satisfaction'!

There's a lighter side to it too – for instance the joy of a schoolgirl whose warts simply dropped off her hands.

Her mother took her to see me, because no medical remedy would rid her daughter's hands of large, unsightly warts. She was teased at school and one teacher actually suggested she should wear gloves in class. She was very upset about it.

Imagine the girl's rapture when, after one visit, within days, the warts started to disappear or drop off. 'Her hands are without a mark now,' her mother confirmed later.

A pretty young girl delivered from an ugly and embarrassing blemish – I think that's a very good reason for rejoicing.

Mrs Pamela Orrell, a Doncaster patient whose eyes were getting very weak, wrote in June 1981: 'I must say my eyes are brilliant these days. It's marvellous to be able to thread a needle without my glasses, and as for my back and stomach trouble, well, I can hardly feel any pain now – it's great.'

She also thanks for the healing her husband received.

He too had stomach trouble which, according to his wife, plagues him no more. I'm still sending him absent healing for breathing difficulties.

The most important aspect of these two people's cures is, I think, contained in a postscript to one of Mrs Orrell's letters: 'You have brought so much happiness into my home also, and so much guidance from spirit. The difficulties I used to have seem a thing of the past now.'

A consultant surgeon, three osteopaths and a chiropractor failed to cure Mr Edwardson of Eastbourne, Sussex, of his 'slipped disc'. He had been in almost constant pain for more than three years.

He became one of my 'instant cure' patients. 'After five minutes in your house I felt immediate relief,' he wrote a month later, adding: 'I'm still free of pain in my back and leg. I can only describe it as a miracle.'

Another patient who spoke of a 'miracle' was Peggy Freedman, who lives in Hove.

Doctors had told her that she suffered from a spinal condition which could be likened to osteo-arthritis and that it could never be cured; that it could be progressive and that all they could do for her was to administer drugs that would dull the pain.

Constant pressure on the sciatic nerve resulted in such agony that pain-killing drugs had little effect. She told me that she had received expert manipulative treatment at a famous London hospital, by one of Britain's foremost specialists in such diseases.

He had not been able to help her and what's more, had held out no hopes for a cure by any of the known orthodox methods.

'With one visit to you,' she said to me later, 'the sciatic nerve was untrapped and an instant change was felt in my spinal cord, and this happened with no obvious pressure.'

Peggy had been one of the desperate cases – envisaging a wheelchair at the end of a long and fruitless search for a medical cure.

Dr Robert had released her – through a single deft movement executed by my hands – from an ordeal that had threatened to ruin her life. 'She'll never again suffer this pain – the nerve is freed,' he commented, at the end of the session.

Elizabeth Grier, also a resident of Hove, was cured not only of her long-standing painful arthritis, but of psoriasis as well. The latter is a skin complaint, which had badly affected this patient's legs, and especially her thighs. The medical profession considers psoriasis to be incurable.

An interesting point in this story is that Elizabeth never told me that she was suffering from psoriasis. She was embarrassed by it and in any case – had she not been told that it was incurable?

Dr Robert, of course, knew. His diagnosis was quick and accurate.

'We'll clear that up too,' I heard him say as he took over and the healing started.

Chapter 8

Canada

On the 3rd of July 1981 Phyllis and I were off on our third
and so far longest visit to Canada.

How is it going to turn out this time? we wondered, as
our 'plane touched down at Calgary. Would we be able to
maintain the success of our first two visits?

We need not have worried. The tour was to become a
triumph from beginning to end.

On arrival we were hardly given time to catch our
breath, so eagerly had we been awaited. We had flown
eight hours from Gatwick airport, where we had taken
off on a typical English summer day: cool and pouring
with rain! At Calgary a solid wall of heat met us as we
stepped off the plane. The temperature was over one
hundred degrees Fahrenheit.

There was absolutely no chance of catching up with
our 'jet lag' or of getting used to the change of climate:
for the next day, a Saturday, a full healing rota had been
booked from midday to 5 o'clock in the afternoon. We
didn't get to bed that night till 1.30 in the morning and
on Sunday afternoon more private appointments had
been made. That night we managed to get to bed by
12.30.

I must admit, by that time I was pretty flaked out and
immensely grateful that our first healing sessions had
gone well; despite jet lag and tiredness they had been
highly successful and I have no doubt that Dr Robert and

every member of his group had helped to supply extra energy.

For the following three days our sponsors had arranged a trip by car to the Rocky Mountains – and now we could relax and unwind.

It was a magnificent experience. The beauty of the landscape through which we drove enthralled us and I can find no adequate words to describe the majesty and overwhelming grandeur of the Rocky Mountains.

We were making for the Ahabasca Glacier and the final ascent was made in a so-called 'snow-mobile', a kind of iron tank, which took us right up to the icefields. We passed Peyto Lake on our way, where you get a fifty mile view along the backbone of the Rockies. It's a famous view, discovered in 1894 by a young mountain guide called Peyto, after whom the place is named. The area is part of the Jasper National Park – a wonderful reserve of Canadian wildlife – and as we drove through forest areas lower down we saw a brown bear ambling along the edge of a wood.

The icefields were of a blinding, blue-white magnificence and if before I had been complaining about the heat, now I was shivering! Well, we were 'on ice', weren't we?

We left the glacier to be taken down to Morain Lake, a lovely mountain resort, where we spent the nights in a chalet.

Every year, in July, a great event called the 'Calgary Stampede', where cowboys show off their horsemanship, takes place, and there's a big fair with all manner of amusements. As we were in Calgary at the time of the 1981 'Stampede' we were taken to see it.

It was great fun. A typical Canadian folk festival, in which everybody in and around Calgary seemed to join with immense gusto and enthusiasm. Cowboys, horses, Indians – it was like a scene from a 'Wild West' film.

We visited the Indians – come from their Reserves to show and sell their wares at the 'Stampede' – in their tents and admired their beautiful woollen knitwear and their artistically worked leathergoods. The wool, which they spin into lengths, is waterproof, because of its high natural oil content. It comes from a particular breed of mountain sheep.

My work was concentrated on Calgary and Victoria. We didn't get to Vancouver this time and a planned visit to USA fell through because we didn't get our visas in time. It was probably just as well, for more patients than I could possibly treat awaited me in Calgary and Victoria.

We were given a charming bungalow for our own use in Victoria. On previous visits we had been staying in an hotel and had been very well looked after, but to have a 'home of our own' this time was very much nicer. It was comfortably furnished and provided with every possible aid to the housewife. Everything was electric, and a 'daily' came in to do the cleaning. Phyllis was delighted.

'All I have to do is push buttons,' she said, 'and everything is arranged in such a practical way – it's a housewife's dream!'

She rarely had to do any cooking, however, for we were usually out for our meals. What particularly charmed us about our bungalow were the little personal touches; like the bunch of flowers, renewed the moment it wilted, so that we were never without a bouquet of magnificent blooms.

As on our two previous visits, the public healing demonstrations in Victoria took place at the Queen Victoria Inn, packed at each occasion.

Billed as 'lectures', they were immensely popular and attracted a great many people interested in psychic healing as such, quite apart from actual patients.

Virginia McCaffrey, an old acquaintance of ours from earlier visits, acted as a commère, giving a short introductory talk and then introducing the patients as they came up for healing. Phyllis, who was on the platform with me, helped with the patients and supervised in a general way.

Virginia gave a 'running commentary' on what was

happening whilst I was healing and afterwards patients who had no objection could speak into the microphone and tell the audience about themselves, their ailments and what they had felt during the healing.

The music I needed to keep me from going into a trance was provided by Daniel, a young guitar player, who gave me exactly the type of music I required.

There were many old friends and patients who came to greet us. Among them was a young couple who proudly showed me their eight-month-old son Terry. They had come to me on my first visit, because they were despairing of ever having a child. Their marriage was a very happy one, but their most fervent wish – a child – had been denied them.

I really didn't know what Dr Robert would think of their plea for help – being childless isn't exactly a disease.

Dr Robert, however, was sympathetic: 'They're unhappy about it – let's try and help them.'

So I had given them healing and little Terry seems to have been the result! Mother and father looked radiant. Their happiness and fulfilment is now complete.

Mrs Jeanette Cowan, a lady who lives in Victoria, simply couldn't believe the 'miracle' that happened to her. She had arrived at Queen Victoria Hall with a badly curved spine. She had always had it and had suffered greatly, mentally and physically, from what she called 'my crooked back'.

It was straightened after one short healing, and it happened then and there, in full view of the audience: Jeanette Cowan rose from the patient's stool with a straight back.

At another public demonstration in the same hall, Mr Riding, also from Victoria, was cured of Emphysema, a chronic disease of the lungs, which had plagued him since 1947. The symptoms of Emphysema are very distressing. There's an abnormal pressure of air in the lungs, which causes the sufferer pain and makes him struggle for breath; even a severe attack of bronchitis could not produce the same, appalling, discomfort.

*

There had been no advance publicity of my visit – it hadn't been necessary: the news had travelled far and wide, spread mostly through former patients by word of mouth, and 'new' healings brought more patients in their wake.

Mrs Joan Shaw, a private patient from Duncan BC, made an appointment for treatment of her arthritic back and her eye-trouble. The result of her healing session was so positive that her husband, who was in great pain from a trapped sciatic nerve, followed in her footsteps and also came over from Duncan. He received immediate relief from pain as Dr Robert released the nerve.

'This is the end of your problem,' I told him. 'The nerve is free and you'll no longer suffer even a twinge of pain.'

Well, his 'on the spot cure' resulted in a veritable avalanche of requests for bookings even from places as far away as Winnipeg and Saskatoon.

At one point I had thirty-five people on 'stand-by' – waiting for cancelled appointments, and by the time we left I had seen well over two hundred Canadian and American patients.

Appearing in a radio programme and two TV shows gave me tremendous publicity and I don't know what I would have done without the help of the Chrysalis Spiritual Development Society, Victoria. They agreed to have telephone calls relayed to their office to take the pressure off me, booked private healing appointments and arranged public healing demonstrations and social events.

On July 15th I appeared on the Terry Spence and Bev Sinclair radio show in a half hour interview on spiritual healing and how it works. Exactly 'how' psychic healing works nobody rightly knows. It involves much that cannot be explained in three-dimensional terms; but I could give listeners some indication of the way in which healing forces are transmitted to the patient via the healer, and explain about Dr Robert Koch and the role he and other spirit helpers play in the healing process.

The next event was the 'Ida Clarkson TV Chat Show'

on July 22nd. I was booked to appear for nine minutes; but Ida Clarkson – a most charming and attractive lady – became so intrigued with the subject, which was new to her, that the show overran. I had given her my scrapbook of cases, so that she could pick out some particularly interesting ones to talk about, and at one point she held the book up to the camera for close-ups.

The show was a huge success and, as was to be expected, resulted in another flood of requests for healing. It all worked out surprisingly smoothly, thanks to the Chrysalis Society dealing with the queries. I was delighted when the TV station gave me a video tape of the show to take home to Britain.

My third media appearance, this time a TV phone-in programme on 'Channel X', caused a sensation. It happened on August 7th and was hosted by Linda Hardy.

Linda had been a patient who had come to me with a cyst on the right hand side of her jaw. It was a parallel case to my own, when I had to have that giant cyst removed by an operation at Guy's Hospital, London. Linda's cyst may not have been as big as mine, but basically she was facing the same ordeal; but in her case Dr Robert dispersed the growth completely in two healing sessions.

The person who usually hosts phone-in programmes on Channel X knew absolutely nothing about Spiritualism, spiritual healing or any other psychic matters; so Linda, who is a Spiritualist and a member of the Chrysalis Society and knows the subjects well, was asked to take over.

She did it with great efficiency and charm. As an introduction, she was to ask me some general questions, but she had to give up and open the lines to the public after the fourth question, as the phones were already jammed with eager callers clamouring to get through to me. In Britain phone-ins are, as far as I know, done only on radio; this one seemed to delight people more, because they could see as well as hear me.

The interest was immense. Not much is known in Canada about psychic matters. Questions on Spiritualism, mediumship, healing and particularly on attitudes to such subjects in Britain simply poured in.

Inquirers were friendly, intelligent, and very open-minded. Among the fifty-five people who got through to me was only one unsympathetic caller: a lady, who was downright hostile and offensive.

'You must be in league with the powers of darkness,' she informed me and asked how much I charged for my 'infernal services'.

I didn't get a chance to answer her, for Linda took over, apologised to me for the lady's rudeness, explained that I never charged fees – neither here nor in Britain – and handed the line over to the next caller, who apologised all over again for the lady's 'uncalled for and unjustified attack'.

Here, as well as on the Ida Clarkson Show, people may have been somewhat surprised to hear that a 'spirit doctor' who in earth life had been a famous German scientist and physician, was actually healing through me; but, apart from that one exception, there was no scoffing or ridicule, only genuine – if sometimes a little puzzled – interest.

The 'phone-in was scheduled to last from 9 to 10 pm, but at close-down the 'phones wouldn't stop ringing, so I was taken to an ante-room off the set, where I took calls for almost another hour.

Daphne Good, the station's manageress, was rapturous with delight.

'What a success! This station has never seen anything like it,' she beamed and presented me with a video cassette of the whole show.

What's more, the three camera men involved came to me for healing! None of them had anything seriously wrong with them, but they presented their ills – I cannot remember what they were now – with touching confidence and gratitude. They told me that several repeats would be given of 'that great show'.

112

*

Among my private patients was the head of a Calgary stone mason's firm, Mr Wayne D Devitt, who had been troubled by a steadily worsening back condition for five-and-a-half years.

Medics had termed his complaint a 'mechanical insufficiency of the lower lumbar spine, accompanied by facet degenerative disease'. He had sought help from doctors, specialists, osteopaths and chiropractors, none of whom had been able to relieve his pain, let alone cure him.

As the condition worsened, he became less and less able to conduct his business. Work turned into agony and so did leisure. The excruciating pain gradually became unbearable. At times less severe than at others, it was nevertheless constant and slowly wore him down. Sometimes the pain intensified to a point where he could not stand, nor find relief in any other position; even the pain-killing drugs prescribed by his doctor could not alleviate his suffering.

He had heard about me and my work in what he described as his 'darkest hour'. His work and business were faltering, due to lack of time spent on the job and because, in the fearful depression that had engulfed his spirit, he could not concentrate his thoughts on any of the problems confronting him.

'I've come to see you thinking that it couldn't possibly hurt and might perhaps help,' he confessed to me at the time of his first treatment.

A most touching letter of acknowledgement, testifying to his cure, arrived when Phyllis and I were back in Britain.

'I am living proof that you have healed me,' he writes. 'I thank God for guiding me to you, as I have never felt as well since the first back pain I experienced. After days and years without a pain free moment, I am now just that – pain free. Unbelievable! I work every day now and mentally I feel a new person.

'I am eternally grateful to you, Mr Pilgrim, and thank

you from the bottom of my heart for sharing your gift with me, God bless you.'

Mary Reilly, a young woman of twenty-two and mother of a baby girl, belongs to the rare cases where a cancer cure was achieved.

As I've mentioned before, cancer is one of the most difficult diseases to heal, but progress is being made. Dr Robert has told me of the great efforts made in the spirit world to find ways of dealing with this scourge of mankind.

'Man will not find a cure as long as he misuses animals in cruel experiments in his research laboratories. This is not the way. Never will health be found by the torture of creatures who are "man's lesser brethren". Nature will provide the answer when man has learnt to live by the laws of the Great Spirit.'

This is the teaching of the spirit guide known as 'Silver Birch', whom I have mentioned in Chapter 5. Dr Robert agrees with him.

Mary Reilly had no great hopes when she arrived for her first appointment. Her doctor had diagnosed an 'active uterine cancer' and she had decided to come and see me before submitting to an operation. She was very depressed, but listened attentively to all I told her about spirit healing and my 'spirit doctor'.

When I told her after the last healing session that Dr Robert wanted to assure her that the cancer had completely disappeared, she brightened considerably, but was not one hundred per cent convinced.

To her immense joy her doctor, as well as his laboratory, confirmed what they almost refused to believe: the cancer had indeed vanished.

The hospitality Phyllis and I received was as extensive as on our previous visits.

Wherever we went we were invited and entertained; asked to luncheon and dinner parties, taken to film shows and to the theatre, where we saw – of all things – Agatha Christie's thriller 'The Mousetrap'!

Victoria, where we spent the greater part of our time,

lies near the sea and has a picturesque harbour where large vessels from Seattle and Port Angeles can dock, and small, privately owned sailing craft anchor along the quays. We saw all the sights of the town, but liked the harbour area best.

Towards the end of our stay friends took us on a weekend trip to Yellow Point, a seaside resort. Along the drive there – about three hours by car – was sheer joy. We had perfect weather, not too hot, with a breeze blowing from the sea and the countryside bathed in sunlight; quite a contrast in its gentle loveliness to the wild beauty of the Rocky Mountains.

Yellow Point itself was enchanting, and Phyllis was out very early the first morning, taking photographs.

'This place has a magic,' she said, and now we're back home she told me that when she wants to meditate and seeks a mood of utter tranquillity, she thinks herself back to Yellow Point in the very early morning.

We sunbathed, swam, went for drives, had our lunch out in the open near the sea and spent the nights in a true Canadian log cabin.

Yellow Point has hot springs – good for rheumatism. You sit in a tub called a 'Jacuzzi' and soak in the healing waters. Of course we had to sample that too.

There were a great many farewells to be made in Victoria and Calgary before we left Canada. Friends and patients came to say goodbye and wish us luck and healing sessions went on right to the end.

Our friends in Victoria arranged a big farewell party at our bungalow before we were off to Calgary and on September 10th we boarded our plane back to Britain.

It had been an interesting, enjoyable and from a healing point of view, highly successful trip.

However, something that happened back home whilst we were away cast a shadow of deep sadness into our hearts.

On July 17th I found myself thinking almost constantly and with ever mounting anxiety of my old friend and mentor, Maurice Barbanell, the editor of *Psychic News*.

'Barbie', as all his friends called him, had been a

constant friend and ally in good and bad times. He had helped me when I had been let down by people I trusted, had smoothed my path as a healer, defended me against unfair criticism, and he and his wife Sylvia – a gifted writer and poet – had shared many happy hours with Phyllis and me at our present Brighton home and before we moved there had stood by us in all the troubles connected with our damp abode at Sackville Gardens, Hove.

By the evening of the 17th my anxiety had become so great that I decided to ring the Barbanell's London flat.

We sat up until after midnight because of the eight hour difference in time between Canada and Britain, and put a call through at about 8 am London time.

The telephone rang a long time before it was answered and I heard Sylvia's voice on the line.

She was utterly bewildered, had no idea who was calling and couldn't understand anything I said.

'My husband died yesterday afternoon,' she said in a flat, toneless voice.

It was impossible to talk to her. She was in such a state of shock that nothing I or Phyllis said sank in. When she replaced the receiver she still had no idea to whom she had been speaking.

Phyllis and I were stunned; unable to take in what we had heard. Neither of us could sleep that night and about 9.30 London time we rang the *Psychic News* office and spoke to Tony Ortzen, the associate editor, who confirmed the sad news.

'But how on earth did you know about this?' he asked.

I told him about my strong sense of foreboding and how it had got so overwhelming that I had rung the Barbanell's flat earlier in the morning.

'I heard Sylvia's distraught voice over the phone – she could do no more than state the stark fact.'

Tony informed me that Maurice Barbanell had died of a heart attack about 6 pm London time, on July 17th at the age of seventy-nine.

To Sylvia the loss is irreparable; Barbie and Sylvia had been the most united couple I think I ever met. They were truly 'one' and would have celebrated their golden wedding anniversary – fifty years of a supremely happy marriage – in 1982.

Spiritualism's loss is doubled by the fact that Maurice Barbanell was not only the founder and editor of *Psychic News*, the world's most widely read Spiritualist weekly paper, and the author of many books on psychic subjects, but also the medium of 'Silver Birch', whose voice on this earth has also been silenced.

So it had been something like a gift from heaven when Phyllis and I had been invited to one of the famous Hannen Swaffer Circle meetings shortly before we left for Canada. It was to be the last meeting of its kind.

Our first sitting in 1977 had deeply impressed us and we were particularly happy to be able to listen to Silver Birch before setting out on our trip.

It was a sitting at which, apart from Phyllis and myself, some of the Barbanell's closest friends were present; among them Lady Michaela Denis-Lindsay, on a visit to London from her home in Nairobi, Kenya, whom many will remember as the star of the Armand and Michaela Denis television series 'On Safari', and Joe Benjamin, one of Britain's most famous mediums and his wife Kitty.

'You still have plenty of work to do,' said Silver Birch when he turned to Phyllis and me. 'You heard me tell Kitty and Joe (Benjamin) that they were brought together to do this work; it applies to you too. It took a long time and there were many difficulties in the way, problems to be solved, many heartbreaks to be endured before it could take place but that belongs to the closed pages of the book (of life) – yes?

'The only value of the past is that it is the pattern of the present and the future; it has lessons to teach, it is part of the tapestry of earthly life and all its threads play their part in framing a pattern which will emerge and show that it is based on a unity and harmony of purpose.

'I said to Joe that the Great Spirit had bestowed the gift of the spirit on him, and the same was done for you.'

When I told him I felt very privileged he countered: 'It

is not only a privilege, it is also a great responsibility. You see, you are the receptacle, the channel, the vessel, the instrument through which the divine power of life itself flows; the power that can perform what others regard as miracles and provide health where there is sickness and give hope where individuals fear there could be no hope for them; that is a wonderful task to perform ...

'What you do clergymen cannot do, priests and rabbis cannot do unless they possess similar powers. But you know, the Great Spirit, with wisdom that is often incomprehensible and seemingly mysterious to your world, bestows his gifts not on those who think they should possess them but on those whom infinite wisdom decides should be their possessors.'

When I was asked if I had any questions, I told Silver Birch that I had had two patients recently, suffering from the same illness.

'One was completely cured,' I explained, 'but the other one never responded to the healing. Why is this? Is it that the particular person is not ready?'

'Yes,' he answered. 'You see, every happening has its purpose, there are no accidents, no coincidences, only planned operations, laws of cause and effect at work. At some stage in human life the Great Spirit provides his children with an opportunity not only of finding themselves, but of achieving self-realisation, and to do so the soul has to be touched.

'Now if the soul is not touched, the power of the spirit cannot work there and if a cure is achieved and the soul not touched, then the healing has failed in its purpose also. The whole object of our return to your world is to demonstrate spiritual reality so that people will stop chasing shadows and learn what are the basic fundamental truths on which all life is based.

'The power that streams through you was available to both, one responded, the other one did not.'

'It made me very sad,' I said.

'Of course it is sad, but it is sad for them,' he countered. 'You cannot heal them all, there are some who will never be cured in your world; they are paying karmic debts and have lessons to learn and the healing will not touch them. So that is why I say: do the best you can; you are there to be available. What happens after you have done the healing is not your responsibility. You have to provide the best conditions, to be the purest channel, reach out to the highest you can attain. That is your responsibility, but remember that you are helping souls to find themselves that otherwise would not have done so. Just go forward, welcome the task that each day brings and rejoice that you can continue to be the channel for the greatest power in the universe.'

Touching on my Canadian venture, he said: 'You are embarking on another mission in a land that is not unfamiliar to me, so I have a great interest in it and you will be provided with many opportunities for serving.'

'I would feel very comforted if I thought you would be around,' I said.

'Oh yes, I will be around,' he assured me.

He had something of import to say to each visitor; something that had a bearing on the private concerns of the person he was talking to and was at the same time of universal interest.

To Lady Michaela, who has strong mediumistic gifts and at that time faced problems concerning her own private circle in Nairobi, he said: 'It was not by accident that you were taken to the land where you dwell. Conditions are difficult at present, it is a maelstrom, but good will emerge. Lessons are to be learnt and you will be guided as you have been guided for many years. You will triumph because you have much work to do in the land where you live ...

'A way will be found for you to be able to dispense the healing and the comfort, the guidance which can help people in a land where the power of the spirit has very few bridges ...

'You are surrounded by much love; you are aware of it; you have protection. The way will be shown.'

To Joe Benjamin, whose high reputation as a medium rests on his ability to furnish proof of life after death:

'You have helped many to replace their tears of sorrow with the smile of certainty; you have brought them knowledge when they thought knowledge was unobtainable; you have enabled love to be reunited with its beloved, provided guidance for those who thought there was no way to turn – and you still have work to do.'

Joe Benjamin had spoken of material difficulties to be overcome.

'I do not have to tell you that the channels, the instruments of the Great Spirit must not expect a bed of roses, that is not their way,' said Silver Birch.

'They have to meet with real difficulty and challenge. We cannot promise you that you will live in the lap of luxury; that would not be good for you, but all that you require will be provided, the wherewithal will be available for you. Just continue to uplift those who come to you.'

And when Benjamin said: 'Almost all the people who used to help me have passed – I seem to have outlived them,' he answered: 'They are still with you, they have not left you; physically, yes, spiritually, no. You have a mighty band, some of whom you have never seen, who come to you to help, so that you can continue the service that has enriched the lives of many people.'

'Would you say that in the olden days the prophets were the mediums of the times?' asked Joe.

'Yes, of course,' came the answer. 'They were persecuted by the priests and priestcraft won – the prophets lost; but this time the prophets are winning and the priestcraft losing.

'We are here to perform many tasks in your world. We have still to root out a lot of ignorance and have still to demonstrate the supreme reality of the spirit.'

To an old friend, a journalist who had just come back from abroad, where things had gone badly for her, he said: 'Life is a polarity, action and reaction; equal and opposite, they are the two sides of the same coin. Every aspect can be used for good or ill – that is the element of choice, your free will. That is the tribute that the Great Spirit has conferred on you so that you are able to make decisions and not be mere puppets or marionettes ...

'You have free will to make your decisions and we try to guide you as much as we can so that you make the right ones. Sometimes we have to let you go your own way to learn lessons, but we know that you will emerge unscathed and you will add to the score of your experience. You must endure hardship and tribulation, you must have the challenge, face the obstacles and the handicaps, otherwise the tremendous latent divinity within you will never find expression.

'You have a tremendous reservoir within yourselves that is seldom tapped and certainly very infrequently utilised. There was a great soul in your world who was called to lead his country at a time of one of its greatest crises and he told the millions listening to him: "You have nothing to fear but fear itself." Fear is the shadow, not the reality. Have no fear, bask in the sunlight of knowledge.'

The philosophy of the great and mysterious soul known as Silver Birch has been my guiding principle for more years than I care to count and the story of my life up to date would be incomplete without some homage paid to the influence this has had on my thinking. It is for this reason that I have quoted these short excerpts from the last of the famous Silver Birch circle meetings.

To Phyllis and me the loss of 'Barbie' – bringing with it the loss of Silver Birch – is doubly grievous, as it must be to countless Spiritualist and non-Spiritualist friends of both these great souls.

Phyllis had taken a tape of Silver Birch speaking through his medium with her on our trip and when we were driving through the glorious country of the Rocky Mountains on our outing to the icefields, chauffeured by one of our generous hosts in a large, comfortable Cadillac, she played the tape.

'I thought it would be nice to listen to him in the land that at some time in the past had been his own.'

It was, in fact, quite magical. At that point we had no idea that we should never again hear Silver Birch's or Barbie's voice – except on tape.

Remembering his assurance that he would 'be around' on our Canadian trip, I closed my eyes and listened with concentrated attention.

It occurred to me later that it might, well have been Silver Birch who prepared me for the shock of Barbie's sudden passing by impressing me with that feeling of restless anxiety that befell me on July 17th.

There were certainly occasions when I could feel his nearness; mostly out in the open – the lonelier the spot, the stronger the feeling of Silver Birch's presence.

Back in England it took us quite a while to settle back into our old routine, but after about a week we had once again got used to a normal home life and our well-tried working schedule.

A friend of ours had been taking our 'phone calls, had opened and answered letters and booked appointments. After nearly three months absence the flood of pleas for healing may be imagined.

Gradually things sorted themselves out, urgent cases were seen to straight away and those of my regular patients who just come for a 'topping up of their batteries' good-naturedly waited until the most pressing problems had been attended to.

It was quite a while after our return, when I was back doing my normal work load, that I 'saw' Barbie.

I was sitting in my favourite armchair, resting and thinking of nothing in particular. Nobody else was in the room. It was very quiet – and suddenly, there he was, standing next to my chair and smiling down at me. He lifted his shoulders and spread out his arms in a typical 'Barbie' gesture.

'You were right,' he said, 'only we didn't think it would happen so soon – did we?'

He was referring to something Dr Robert had once said. Barbie used to come to me as a patient for his eye-trouble.

'You must admit that nobody has helped my eyes as much as Tom has,' he told someone who had criticised me in a rather off-hand manner.

'Barbie will go quite suddenly and in the midst of his work,' Dr Robert had said. 'I think he'd be delighted to know this, because it is the way he would like to go.' Of course, no date or time was given.

When I told Barbie he had been very pleased indeed and had said: 'My God, how wonderful! Isn't it nice to know that one won't be suffering a long drawn out painful illness or perhaps lose one's mental powers and gradually deteriorate? But I suppose we all would like to go swiftly – anyway, I'm grateful to Dr Robert for letting me know.'

'Well,' he said now, raising his eyebrows, 'it was indeed very sudden. At present I'm still learning to adjust to the altered conditions in which I live – and make no mistake, I am very much alive. Adjustment is not all that easy at first. Suddenly rid of the crude matter of one's physical body, one has got to learn to control the very much lighter matter and the far higher vibrations of the astral body; but I have Silver Birch at my side to help me – he is still my guide and friend, and it's wonderful to know him "face to face" now we inhabit the same world!'

He went on to describe some of the beauties of the spirit world: 'They are all that Silver Birch told us – and more.'

His one sadness lay in the fact that he had to leave Sylvia behind, 'but she has her own inner resources and they will see her through. Silver Birch and I will look after her until, one day, we are reunited. Love always conquers.'

Chapter 9

Wider Implications

Some cases just ring your heart, especially when you know from the start that a cure is impossible, and the best a sufferer can hope for is alleviation of pain.

Yes, even spirit healing has its limits and it would be dishonest to deny this.

Such a case was the lady from Eastbourne, taken to see me by her daughter. Two wonderful people of indomitable spirit.

They arrived by car and it was obvious at first glance that it would be very difficult to get the patient safely into my sanctuary. Not only was she crippled with arthritis, but she had been given prolonged cortison treatment, which had produced terrible side effects. Her whole body was swollen, her limbs blown up beyond recognition. Her daughter thought the best way would be to let her walk slowly up the path to our back door with the help of her zimmer (a walking aid) and straight into the sanctuary.

We managed to get her out of the car and on to the path. It was a sight to cut into your soul. Her poor puffed out hands turned white from the effort to cling to the zimmer. Step by step she valiantly hobbled along the narrow path on aching legs. It wasn't far and we thought she would make it, when suddenly she got stuck. She couldn't move forward nor back – and with all that she still smiled! A lady in her sixties now, she must have been a beauty in her youth; her eyes, her smile, the whole of her face still bore a sweetness of expression that no suffering had been able to destroy.

She could not hear what we were saying, because apart from all her other handicaps she was also stone deaf, but her daughter could communicate with her. They had their own language and it was heart-warming to see the loving care the daughter lavished on her helpless mother. With infinite patience and gentleness she made it clear to her that it would be best to get her back to the car. It was still nearer than our back door.

Our combined efforts got the lady back in the end, and I gave her healing in the car. The agonies this gentle soul has had to endure are hard to imagine. When I touched her hand I could see the veins breaking beneath the skin. Wherever you put the slightest pressure bruises would appear; there was no firm flesh left anywhere. To ease the pain in her legs and feet and to give them healing we took off her shoes: where the strap had lain across the instep the puffed up flesh was deeply indented; it almost looked as if the foot had two separate halves.

Phyllis was terribly upset. I could see that she was weeping and trying to hide it, and I must admit to having been pretty close to tears myself.

Dr Robert sadly shook his head. 'It has gone too far,' I heard him say. 'If she had come before instead of after the cortisone treatment we could have succeeded. Too late now – all we can do at this stage is to alleviate pain.' I could see how distressed he was and I was dimly aware of Dr Heinemann, who helps with rheumatism and bone disease cases, also being around. I had to keep a firm hold on myself in order not to go into trance as Dr Robert made my hands move gently, gently over the lady's limbs. I hardly touched her, but felt the healing power streaming through my fingers into her tortured body.

I don't think I could ever forget this particular patient – nor her daughter. The case itself must rank among the most heartbreaking I have come across; but what makes it so memorable is the way in which the stricken lady bears her fate. Still smiling, still cheerful she has kept her heart and soul free of despair, resentment or bitterness. The love of her daughter is all this lady has, but it is a gift that will compensate her for all her sufferings right up to the end. What an example in a world so full of selfishness and cruelty, where the old and infirm are so often pushed away into institutions by their children – out of sight and sometimes even out of mind.

Healers often wish patients would not come to them as the very last, desperate resort.

A patient with cancer of the throat came to me in the very last stages of that dreadful disease. A charming lady, also accompanied by her daughter.

Again Dr Robert could only shake his head. The patient had received radiation treatment which had burnt her throat and the skin around the whole area was a mottled black and brown. 'What a shame she did not come earlier – we might have been able to do something in the earlier stage; before radiation was used.'

No spiritual healer and no spirit guide likes to see the side effects of radiation treatment. Radiation tends to kill the healthy cells together with the diseased ones and the healer has nothing left to work on.

'She will pass in a short time,' said Dr Robert. 'It will be a blessed release.'

I know that he will ease her passing when the time comes and in the meantime he will keep her free of pain. We have heard from the daughter since their visit and she told us that her mother is now able to sleep – which she couldn't before – and she can also take a little liquid nourishment. She has been relieved of pain and is in a quiet frame of mind.

Phyllis had told the daughter that not all patients can be healed. She now accepts that in her mother's case a cure would not be possible and expressed her gratitude for the relief the healing had brought her mother.

What always astounds both Phyllis and myself is the trust and confidence displayed by patients who come from afar. Some will travel many miles by car, train or

126

bus, often in very uncomfortable conditions, facing tiresome changes and delays on train journeys, or endless hold-ups on crowded roads. Nothing will deter them.

A new patient, a blind young girl, came with a companion all the way from Leeds by train and bus and went back home the same day.

The girl had a quite unshakable faith that I could help her. When I pointed out that there were healers in her area and going to one in Leeds would save her a long, uncomfortable journey, she said no, it was me, Tom Pilgrim, she wanted, because she had heard of someone I had healed.

A patient suffering from arthritis comes from the Isle of Wight for her healing appointments – also travelling back the same day.

Another, a young woman of twenty-one, who had received the wrong medical treatment for some long standing back trouble, came from Kidderminster. She had been in pain for years. When she rose from the stool in my sanctuary the pain had gone. It was an instant cure.

'I'll sing all the way back to Kidderminster,' she said.

Thinking of patients who take so much trouble to get to me, not to mention those from abroad, it strikes me as rather humorous when some people here in Brighton and Hove complain about having to take two buses to come here!

A letter from a patient acknowledging a cure always brings joy to a healer's heart.

'It's a long time ago that I came to see you and promised to write to you, and I apologise for being so long in getting round to doing so,' writes Ann Black in a letter I received recently.

She had come to see me in 1979, after being told that she was suffering from leukaemia. Her story is one of great suffering and endurance – but with a happy ending.

A healthy young woman in her thirties with two teenage sons, ill health had never touched her until, in 1979, she started feeling out of sorts, tired, listless – 'not at all like my true self,' as she put it. She had a part-time secretarial job in a solicitor's office and, as a qualified Yoga teacher, gave Yoga-classes in the evenings.

She didn't take much notice of her 'run-down state of health', took a tonic and went on with life as usual until one day she simply collapsed. 'I was making the beds when I suddenly keeled over!'

There followed the usual sickening tests, first at the Sussex County Hospital, Brighton, and later at the Royal Marsden Hospital, which specialises in cancer cases.

'It came like a bombshell when they told me I had leukaemia. It was such a shock that I couldn't stop shaking for nearly two hours,' she told me later.

Leukaemia is a comparatively painless disease, the patient gradually getting weaker and weaker, but modern medical treatment of leukaemia is anything but painless. It is also very 'lonely', because the patient's white blood cells, which combat infection, can no longer do their work. This means that any infection, even a very minor one, could seriously affect the patient; so the unfortunate sufferer is kept in strict isolation until, with treatment, the body starts to create new, healthy white cells.

'The worst part of the treatment was the radiation. All my hair fell out,' she wrote later in an article for the magazine *Yoga*; 'I had to wear a wig for quite a long time, but now my hair is growing again and is at present a mass of short, tight curls.'

In her recent letter to me she writes: '... when all my friends and Yoga pupils heard of my plight, they got together in their different groups and concentrated and meditated for me. My Yoga teacher told me that another pupil of hers, Elisabeth Tate, had been coming to you and had great faith in you. She told you about me and it was arranged that you would try healing me.

'I was told that you would think of me at 9.30 am and 10.30 pm and that I should try at these times to also be relaxed and in a meditative state, although this was not particularly necessary, as it would not have mattered had I been asleep. However, I did manage this in the evenings, and on several occasions when in considerable pain, I could feel energy flowing into me and a glow of warmth would spread through my body, driving out the pain.

'Once I thought I could see a sort of nebulous being hovering over me, which gave me a great sense of security and reassurance. At that time, having been very low, this was a great help. You will recall when I came round to see you after I left the hospital telling me "oh yes, that was Dr Robert. At one time he told me you were almost a goner ... but then he said you were going to be all right."

'The outcome in any event was that in December the doctors said I was "in remission" and that my bone marrow had regenerated (this without the bone marrow transplant which the doctors had said would at some stage be necessary).

'Without wishing to detract from the very wonderful care and treatment I received at the hospital, and help from other people's prayers and meditations, I feel that your help played a vital part in my recovery.'

This case is a wonderful example of spiritual healing, prayer and meditation working together with orthodox medicine to achieve a splendid result. Leukaemia cures are still very rare. Patients receiving orthodox treatment often seem to get better for a while, but then suffer a relapse and die. Spiritual healing has few successes to show as yet when it comes to leukaemia and I still think back with awe to the case of the Brighton man whom Dr Robert cured of this dreadful disease so many years ago.

Does the answer lie in cooperation between medical science and spiritual healing? Many problems remain to be solved; for instance that of radiation, which can produce such dreadful and often fatal side-effects. One thing I'm sure of is that the 'holistic' point of view, which is rapidly gaining ground, is the right one.

The 'holistic' approach takes in the whole human being – mentally, spiritually and physically – instead of just treating the diseased physical part alone.

Mr Beard, a therapist who lives in Eastbourne, gave Ann Black a very interesting back-up meditation. He runs a cancer care group which meets once a fortnight in

Brighton. His treatment consists of inducing a positive, imaginative stream of thought in the patient.

He made a forty minute tape for Ann, which told her about relaxation and how to achieve it – much like Yoga, she thought. Then she had to visualise an army of 'good cells' shaped like carpet slippers marching through her body, eating up the 'bad' cells. Why carpet slipper shaped? She had no idea, but somehow the image seemed right and she found it easy to 'see' these chaps moving up one leg, down the other, up one arm, down the other and so on until they had covered every inch of her body.

There is nothing very extraordinary about this. Matthew Manning, once Britain's answer to Uri Geller's metal bending, today uses his psychic powers for healing; he works with the same 'visualisation technique'. Dr Robert approves of it.

'God's healing power flows through many channels and uses many methods,' he says. 'My way is not the only way.'

A case that gave us much cause for rejoicing was that of 'Rosemary', a patient I had treated in Victoria, who is a very dear friend of Phyllis and myself.

When she came for healing during our last stay in Victoria, we didn't really know what was wrong with her. She just complained of feeling run down and asked if she could have healing for general debility.

Well, the real reason for her wanting healing was that she had a lump in one of her breasts and had been told that it was malignant. She had said nothing about this to anybody, except to one close friend. Phyllis and I had no idea of the seriousness of her case.

Dr Robert, however, went straight to the affected breast, telling me as he did so that this was breast cancer – early stage – and that he could cure it.

At the end of her healing session Rosemary broke down and burst into tears. She cried and cried, and not knowing that Dr Robert had already told me the truth, she confessed the real reason of her plea for healing.

She had been worried stiff when she had discovered the lump and had gone straight to her doctor. The examination confirmed her worst fears. The lump was diagnosed as a cancerous tumour. She was in utter despair. Under no circumstance did she want to have her breast removed – I was her last hope.

Two weeks after Dr Robert's treatment she went back to the hospital for another examination. This time the result was negative. The astonished medical men and their colleagues at the laboratory admitted that there was no trace of cancer. The lump had disappeared.

In October 1981, when we had been back in Britain for about a month, we received a charming letter from Rosemary.

'Tom,' she writes, 'I can never thank you enough for the wonderful healing you gave me. To be free of the lump in my breast is a true miracle ...'

'Good grief! What's happened to you!' exclaimed Phyllis when she opened the door to Richard Goalen, a pleasant young man in his thirties, and a former patient.

Richard's head was hanging down on his left shoulder. 'Please don't laugh! I know this looks too silly for words, but it's really awful – I'm off on my holiday tomorrow and I can't lift my head out of this ridiculous position,' he wailed.

Poor young man – he had been like that for about a week, thinking it would right itself, but of course it couldn't, because some of his neck vertebrae had got themselves locked.

Richard Goalen had come to me for the first time in 1978 with serious back trouble. He was in agony from a slipped disc and lowered himself with great difficulty onto the stool to receive healing.

It was one of Dr Robert's instant cures and Richard rose with his spine in mint condition, the disc back in its place.

He had come to my sanctuary as a great sceptic. Faith? Not a scrap of it, and after his spine was straightened and all the pain had gone in a single healing session, he still waited for some weeks before writing me a letter of acknowledgement.

'I wanted to be sure that the cure was permanent,' he wrote; but his scepticism had turned to a firm conviction of the truth of spirit healing and today he tells anybody willing to listen the story of his 'miraculous' cure.

So now he was back, smiling wryly up at me, his head firmly wedged down to the left. He was full of confidence: 'Can you do it again? It would be nice to be able to go off on holiday with my head held high!'

Dr Robert chuckled as he freed the locked vertebrae. 'We can't leave a nice young man in such an awkward predicament, now can we?'

Richard Goalen, happy, fit and immensely grateful, went off on his holiday – his head held high – and as we haven't heard from him since, we presume that it must have been another 'permanent cure'.

In our busy lives Phyllis and I have little time for the social graces and often regret not being able to see more of our friends and relatives; but we are, both of us, on very close and affectionate terms with the children from our previous marriages and somehow manage to see them quite frequently.

My son, Alan, his wife Ann and my grandson Gary, now eight, also live in Brighton, so there's no difficulty in visiting each other.

Neither my son nor my grandson have inherited any of my psychic gifts, and I always thought that my son wasn't really very interested in such things, but I was wrong.

'I think the work that you do is wonderful, Dad, and that you'll leave something behind when you go – I'll leave nothing,' he said to me not long ago.

That's a lot, coming from Alan, because he's never wanted to talk much about healing or any other psychic matters. I think as a child he must have felt a bit overawed by his grandmother's psychic gifts and by having a psychic father as well, though after my mother's death he saw her twice, sitting on top of the staircase in our old home in College Street. He had been very fond of her and wasn't at all frightened when he saw her. He still sees her sometimes, but rarely.

'Well, son, you've had your evidence in seeing your Granny, haven't you?' I told him and he agreed.

Gary is a lovely, bright young lad, but there's nothing psychic in his make-up. Perhaps it's just as well. He'll be spared the 'slings and arrows' that usually lie in wait for those endowed with psychic faculties. His life will be the easier and if he makes as much of a success of it as Alan has done I'll have no complaints.

Phyllis, like me, has one son from her first marriage, but she has four grandchildren; three boys and a girl, of assorted ages between sixteen and six. The girl is the youngest.

Gerald and Maura, Phyl's son and daughter-in-law and their children are a very happy, united family. They live in Shoreham, Sussex, which isn't too far away from us and Phyllis visits them just as often as she can make it, and sometimes the whole family comes to visit us in Brighton.

Phyllis is very proud of her grandchildren. They're lovely kids, but here again – nobody seems to have inherited Phyllis' strong psychic faculties. As a child her son would accompany her to services at the Spiritualist church, and sometimes he would watch healers at work there. Then, at home, he would give his mother 'healing', imitating the healer's strokes and passes, saying 'there now – your headache has gone'; but interest in Spiritualism petered out when he grew up. It's strange, really, because so many members of Phyllis' family were psychically gifted.

Phyllis' brother, for instance, whose passing had caused her so much grief, had done 'colour healing', a healing method in which colours are used. He had been a great Spiritualist and had shown true interest in my work.

'Tom must be a marvellous person to deserve my

133

sister,' he had said to a friend when Phyllis and I were getting married.

Phyllis' psychic faculties are still very much alive, even though she can spare little time for their development. Connie, her much beloved sister-in-law, who had passed on before our marriage, manifests quite often to her. Sometimes in a very typical and amusing way.

'I was in the kitchen, trying to think what to do with some left-overs,' she told me the other day, 'when I heard Connie's voice say quite distinctively: "boil it up for the chickens!"'

This had been a typical phrase of Connie's in the olden days.

We used to have long chats – Connie, Phyllis and myself – always on Sundays, when I used to spend the day at Phyl's home before we were married. It seems that Connie still likes to be with us on Sundays, because we often feel her presence then and when one of us remarks on it, we say 'well, of course – it's Sunday!'

Auntie Rosie, widow of Phyllis' uncle Richard, came to live with us some years ago, after the death of her husband. She has always been very psychic indeed, though now, at the age of eighty-eight, her psychic perception may no longer be as sharp as in her younger days; but she still 'sees' or 'hears' spirit people at times.

When Doris Stokes, one of Britain's top mediums, came to visit us last year, I took her into the sanctuary at one point to give her healing. She had hardly settled herself on the stool when she said: 'Hang on a minute! There's someone here who says he's "Richard" – no, now he says "Dickie" – and he wants to thank you and Phyllis "for being so good to my Rosie".'

This was a very evidential message, which gave us much pleasure. Phyl's uncle Richard was also known as Dickie, so he gave both names as proof, and it was nice to find that he's around, looking in on his Rosie.

Doris Stokes knew no details about aunt Rosie and had certainly never before heard of Richard or Dickie.

As for Rosie herself, she's a very bright old lady, still enjoying life and we're very happy to be able to offer her a home. She would have been appallingly lonely after her Richard had gone. They had been a very devoted couple.

I'm often asked what my plans for the future are. Well, as I think it necessary to spread knowledge of spiritual healing as far and wide as humanly possible, I would like to do more public demonstrations at home and abroad.

Dr Robert has already told me that before long we shall be visiting Germany. He is naturally very keen to demonstrate his continued existence and his extended healing mission in the country that was once his fatherland.

Gibraltar has invited me twice already, but each time the invitation clashed with some other commitment and I had to decline; but I'm sure that I'll go there one day.

Canada wants me back again, this time for four months – but that would be too long an absence from my patients here in Britain. I think about two months should be the limit.

Throughout my life I have been given proof of spirit guidance, but no incident has been stranger or more compelling than the following. It happened as Phyllis and I were leaving Switzerland after one of our healing demonstrations there, and talking of foreign travel has reminded me of it.

We were travelling from Lugano to Zürich, where we would catch our plane to London. By some mistake we had been put on the wrong train and when the ticket inspector came along he informed us that we would have to change at a place I'd never heard of, which sounded like 'Goulden'. Not knowing the language – we were in the German-speaking part of Switzerland – this was very awkward, but the other people in our carriage had got the gist of what was going on and kindly told us when we had reached the place where we had to change.

We tumbled out of the train, not knowing from which platform and at what time we could catch a train to Zürich. We tried to ask one or two people, but nobody understood us, so we rushed down a staircase leading to an underground passage from which other staircases led up to different platforms. The word 'Zürich' appeared nowhere.

Phyllis ran down the passage in one direction to have a look, I in the other. At the end of my part of the passage one staircase led up to the outside world – I could see traffic passing in the street – another led up to a platform, but there was no indication of departures to Zürich.

I turned round, desperate to find someone who could give me some information, when suddenly a lady's voice behind me called out loudly in German: 'Mein Herr, mein Herr!' I swung round again to face the staircase leading to the street and there, on the third step from the bottom, stood a lady dressed from head to toe in black. I remember vividly that her small feet, just peeping out from beneath her long, black skirt, were clad in shiny patent leather shoes. She wore a black hat with a veil. Her appearance was so striking that every detail has remained in my mind's eye to this day.

As I turned towards her she lifted the veil from her face with one hand – she was a good-looking woman of perhaps thirty or thirty-five – looked at me with an expression of great urgency in her eyes and pointed with the other hand excitedly towards the other staircase, shouting 'Zürich! Zürich!' in a tone of voice which implied 'for God's sake hurry!'

'Oh, thank you, Madam,' I cried, turned to look for Phyllis, spotted her half-way down the passage and waving madly called out 'it's up here, come quickly!' As Phyllis started to run I looked back to where the lady in black had stood in order to thank her again – but the staircase was empty. No trace of anybody. I had only turned from her for a few seconds; it would have been impossible for her to get up all those steps to the street in that time, and if she had come down the last three steps she would have had to pass me in the passage.

The lady had simply vanished; yet she had stood there as solidly three-dimensional as Phyllis was who had now caught up with me. I grabbed her by the arm – the lady in black had infected me with her urgency – and together we

136

raced up to the platform our friendly helper had indicated.

We had hardly arrived at the top of the stairs when a train came in: the carriages were clearly marked Zürich. It only stopped for about two minutes. We had just caught it!

I have no idea who the 'lady in black' was. I have never seen her before or since. She was obviously a spirit being sent to help us, but who sent her? How did she know that we were looking for a train to Zürich? In earth life she must have been German or Swiss and couldn't have been connected with Phyllis' or my family.

Did Dr Robert, knowing of our predicament and being unable to help us himself, send her? Was she a relative or a friend of his who volunteered to appear to me? I simply don't know. When I next saw Dr Robert it was in my sanctuary and we were far too occupied with the healing of our patients to think of anything else and somehow I never got round to asking him.

I get the impression that a great deal of trouble is taken by the spirit world to give us mortals guidance when there is need of it. I have felt it in various ways throughout the whole of my life – most of all during the war. God's guidance seems to come to us through countless channels and sometimes in the oddest ways. It would have been disastrous if we had missed that train, for it would have made us miss our plane to London. We should have been forced to stay in Zürich overnight and healing appointments made for the next day could not have been kept, and there were some serious cases awaiting me.

Whoever that lady in black was, she did us a great service and my thanks go out to her and to whoever it may have been who sent her.

Not so very long ago Spiritualists in Britain ranked with rogues and vagabonds; a medium or a healer could be indicted under the Witchcraft Act of 1735 and sent to prison. Helen Duncan, a medium of world-wide repute was actually killed by the after effects of one such trial.

She was a 'physical' or 'materialisation' medium who possessed the rare gift of being able to produce 'physical phenomena', such as the movement of inert objects, 'apports' (the appearance of objects from seemingly nowhere) and actual, physical materialisation of spirit beings who can be seen, recognised and even touched by ordinary sitters during a seance.

In order to produce these phenomena the medium has to go into a very deep trance, and if such a trance is suddenly and forcefully interrupted, it can prove fatal to the medium. Helen Duncan, torn from deep trance by police breaking into one of her materialisation seances, fell desperately ill, recovered sufficiently to stand trial and was sent to prison. She was released because of her state of health and later died, soon after the police raided her premises for a second time.

She can be called a true martyr to Spiritualism. Not long after her death, and owing to strong pressure from all the Spiritualist organisations and from large sections of the general public, the Witchcraft Act was repealed in 1951.

Since then great progress has been made in Britain. Spiritualism, once banned from radio and television, is now freely discussed in all the media and orthodox medical men cooperate with spiritual healers.

Science world-wide is gradually beginning to open up to an entirely new conception of how the universe is shaped. A multi-dimensional realm beyond the confines of time and space is now considered a serious hypothesis by scientists of repute. The frontiers of knowledge are continuously being extended.

John Hasted, Professor of Experimental Physics and Head of Department at Birkbeck College, London University, mentions in his book *The Metal-Benders* the possibility of a parallel universe, or an infinite number of parallel universes, as an acceptable scientific theory.

Looked at in this light the reality of a 'spirit world' should no longer be so difficult to grasp, and communication with such a world should appear much more natural. Mediums and healers are, after all, no more than especially sensitive human instruments geared to receive the finer, higher, vibrations of that 'other world'.

Our world is sick with many diseases, but spiritual healing can cure people when they are ready for it.

The spirit doctors do the work from their side and the medium is the essential link between the healing force and those who need it; thus the divine healing power is poured down through the spirit world into ours; but only with the extended vision of the spirit guides can be seen exactly what takes place when a sufferer appeals to a medium.

Many of my patients who are healed write and acknowledge their healing. Many more never write at all, but I know that much good is being done, because of the tremendous increase in people writing to me asking to be healed.

As every kind of disease is being treated and men, women and children are restored to health or are sent away with a tranquil mind, a healer is taught humility; for he comes to know that the tear-laden thanks are not a tribute to him as a person, but the soul's expression of joy at having regained the harmony that comes from spiritual as well as from bodily health.

Spiritualism tries to free mankind from the shackles of creeds, dogmas and rituals and to teach the simple truths that life is eternal, that communication between this world and the next is quite natural, and that all can approach God directly, without intervention of priest or church.

A rather pompous parson who doesn't like Spiritualists once said to me: 'How come you can heal and I can't?'

'Because God is no respector of parsons,' I told him. He didn't like my answer, but it's still true.

To me Spiritualism's most endearing features are its lack of pomposity, its bright, positive philosophy, and its encouragement also of the lighter side of life, which allows for a healthy sense of humour.

My old friend Maurice Barbanell, known to his journalist colleagues in Fleet Street as 'Mr Spiritualism', was one of **the** wittiest, most humorous people I've ever known. His personal column in *Psychic News* often ended with an amusing tailpiece. One, which amused me very much at the time, was about a class of small boys who had just been told the story of the Good Samaritan. 'Why do you think the priest and the Levite passed the injured man by on the other side of the road?' asked the teacher.

'Please, Sir,' said bright little Johnny, 'it was because they saw that he had been robbed already.'

No criticism? But of course – there's nothing perfect in this world and Spiritualism has its weaknesses as everything else.

There are mediums and healers who launch themselves upon the public before they are ready for this demanding task. I'm often appalled by the low standard of mediumship in some of our Spiritualist churches, and I'm not talking of frauds. No, fraudulent mediums or healers are soon found out and dealt with. I mean the honest, earnest, gifted souls that climb onto public platforms without the necessary experience.

A public demonstration of clairvoyance demands a fully developed medium who is not put off by a difficult audience or difficult conditions, and the Spiritualist organisations should keep watch and see to it that only mediums who are sure of themselves, their guides and their gifts, are allowed to give public demonstrations.

The same goes for healers. It took me many years of careful preparation, gradually developing my gifts and perfecting the cooperation between Dr Robert and myself, before I realised and accepted all the implications of my healing mission.

All of us, mediums and healers, are here to serve our fellowmen and must never fall short of the high standards expected of us. The spirit world tries to prove through us, their instruments, the truth of spiritual realities, and that is a great privilege and a great responsibility.

Appendix

Dr Robert's Story

I thought it might interest readers to know a little more about my 'healing guide', the famous German physician, scientist and Nobel Prize winner Dr Robert Koch and his life on earth.

When the journalist who interviewed me in 1979 asked me about him, Dr Robert had obligingly appeared and given some details of his life and career. They were, however, just bare dates, given to prove his identity. I have described the interview at the end of Chapter 4.

Once I had learnt how famous the man was who had chosen me as his medium, I tried to find out more about him; but the information I found in encyclopaedias and medical text books, though highly interesting to medical students, did not make very enthralling reading for the layman.

Dr Robert knows I'm writing this book and is pleased about it, because it is part of his mission to spread knowledge and appreciation of spirit healing, and the book should help to do just that.

I now needed some interesting material about his life and I had no idea where to find it. There are some excellent German publications but, not knowing the language, they wouldn't help me. A certain amount I knew from what Dr Robert had told me himself, but I needed more information and I couldn't expect him to sit down and go through his whole life with me – he is a busy man in his own sphere. Browsing round in libraries in the hope of finding something suitable was too time consuming – so I was stuck.

I had put the whole idea out of my mind for the time being, when a patient who is also a friend, walks into my sanctuary waving a book.

'Look what I've found,' she says and hands me an old book bound in blue linen entitled *Bouquet For The Doctor*, by Dorothy Fisk, in a 1955 edition of the Scientific Book Club.

'Turn to page 190,' says my friend. 'I think you'll find that Chapter 11 will interest you.'

I do as she says and there, before my eyes, is exactly what I've been looking for: Chapter 11 is the story of Dr Robert Koch, his life and his work, written in a pleasant, easy to read style.

My friend beams. 'Isn't that great?' she asks. 'I came upon it quite by chance in a shop that sells a lot of old books. It was among some cheap ones on display. Don't ask me why I picked it out – I don't even know why I went into that shop; just idle curiosity I suppose, but when I had pulled the book out, it opened at Chapter 11! Seeing the name of Dr Robert Koch and realising it was his life's story, I bought it for you, because I was sure you would like to have it.'

I was staggered! The lady who had so kindly purchased the book for me had no idea that I was actually looking for literature on Dr Robert's life. She knew I was writing my autobiography, but no more.

Thanking her profusely, I told her how I had toyed with the idea of including the story of Dr Robert Koch in my book, but had almost dropped it because of the problem of finding the right material.

'My goodness,' she answered, 'now I understand my strange compulsion to enter that shop. It was very odd, because I went straight up to the right shelf and pulled out that particular book. Dr Robert must have guided me to it!'

So it seems that Dr Robert has done his best to get me the material I need and wants me to go ahead with my idea.

Here then, is a short account of his life and work on earth.

His full name was Heinrich Hermann Robert Koch, but he was known throughout his life simply as Robert Koch. He was born December 11, 1843 in Clausthal, a small mining town in the Harz mountains, Germany (now East Germany), where his father, a highly intelligent and much respected citizen, was employed as a mining engineer.

Robert was the third of seven children. Home life, happy if a little crowded, was not a life of luxury, but the family suffered no lack of reasonable comforts; the children all received a good education, and Robert stayed at the Clausthal 'Gymnasium' (high school) until he was nineteen. He had inherited his father's high intelligence and at the age of five astonished his family by teaching himself to read – totally unaided, using newspapers as his learning aid. The concentration and perseverance he displayed at that tender age stayed with him for life and was one of the character traits that led to his outstanding successes in research.

Apart from an above average intelligence, Robert had also inherited a great love of travel from his father and thinking that philology might provide opportunities for travelling abroad, he decided to take it as his subject when he went to university; but the headmaster at his school dissuaded him. He didn't think that Robert's talent lay in that direction.

Undecided about what to do, Robert went off to Hamburg to visit an uncle after he had left school. He was fascinated by this great sea port and looked longingly at the big ocean going vessels in the harbour. In the end, however, he followed his headmaster's advice and selected mathematics and science as his subjects at Göttingen University; but after two terms he knew what he wanted and changed over to medicine.

Professor Henle, the anatomy professor at Göttingen, liked the able young student and made him his assistant at the Pathological Museum. Robert did well at

143

university. He enjoyed his studies, and an essay he wrote, which entailed a great deal of research, won him a prize. Research had already begun to fascinate him.

He took his medical degree in 1866 and then went to Berlin, where he absolved the customary six months course in pathological anatomy under Virchow, then the leading pathologist and a famous name throughout Europe. Not feeling at all inclined to settle down in a medical practice, but longing for the great wide world, he thought of going to sea as a ship's doctor. As a first step towards realising this plan he accepted a post at one of the Hamburg hospitals, where he could keep an eye on the shipping companies and would be on the spot if a vacancy occurred.

It was to take a very long time before his desire for world-wide travel could be satisfied. The first thing which prevented him putting his plans into operation was – love. He was by now engaged to his boyhood sweetheart, Emmy Fraatz, who refused point blank when he suggested they should travel together abroad. Her ideas of happiness centred round a home and a settled way of life. Loving her, Robert gave in and after their marriage in 1867 the couple settled in Langerhagen, where Robert became physician to the district asylum. He also built up a private practice, doing his visiting rounds on horseback, which he hugely enjoyed.

Country doctors were not very well paid anywhere in Germany in those days and Robert's financial rewards in Langerhagen were meagre. He moved to Nymegen, a German border town which today lies in Holland, but things proved to be no better there. One of his brothers had emigrated to the USA, and Robert was very tempted to do the same. It would have pleased his adventurous spirit – but once again the home loving Emmy, who was horrified at the idea, put her foot down and once again Robert gave in. Probably to the benefit of mankind, for a career in the USA might have taken him in a different direction, away from research.

So instead of America, the couple's next port of call was Rackwitz – today a Polish town, but then German.

Robert had hardly settled there when the Franco-Prussian war broke out in 1870. He joined the Prussian forces as a field surgeon, but it was a short campaign, ending in 1871 with a swift German victory. Before long Robert was back in Rackwitz.

Sure that he could do better, he now applied for the post of District Physician in Wollstein, and after passing the necessary exams with distinction, he was accepted.

The family stayed in Wollstein for nearly ten years. Robert had a little daughter by now, Gertrud, whom he loved dearly. They were the first truly successful years, and laid the foundation stone not only for Robert's own career, but also for the great advances that were to be made in bacteriological research.

Robert was now fully stretched. He was in charge of two hospitals and his private practice grew so rapidly that two other doctors left – there was no work for them. Everybody wanted to consult this new, brilliant young physician and there were only about four thousand potential patients in the district anyway; but the real significance of the Wollstein years lay in the research Robert did during that time.

Life must have posed quite a few problems to the Koch family. The four-roomed flat they occupied housed not only father, mother and daughter, but also a host of rabbits, mice and frogs, which Robert needed for his research. Today, in the world he now inhabits, he no longer agrees with the practice of animal experiments, but in his days on earth he knew no other way; it was the accepted method.

What Robert Koch achieved in Wollstein was a stupendous achievement, for without specialised training, laboratory or sophisticated equipment, he managed to complete one of the most important research programmes of the nineteenth century. He divided one room in the flat by a curtain, one side to serve as laboratory, the other as a consulting room. The

145

microscope – a much cherished present from Emmy – had to stand near a window where the light was good, and a cupboard, heated by an oil stove, had to be used for Dr Koch's cultures. A dissecting table and some means of sterilising instruments also had to be accommodated.

In these cramped conditions and with the most primitive aids, Dr Robert accomplished the research which demonstrated beyond all doubt that the origin of splenetic fever lay in the anthrax bacillus.

Splenetic fever was a cattle disease which plagued the district in which he lived and occasionally men tending the cattle would catch it with fatal results. Robert started his inoculation experiments with small animals, mostly mice or rabbits, which he accommodated in his makeshift laboratory or – to Emmy's dismay – in the kitchen; but his experiments soon evolved into something more sophisticated. From animals he turned to cultures for his research, which gave him better results in the long run, but he could never do entirely without animals.

One question that puzzled him was how the disease could arise in conditions which actually destroyed the micro-organisms that caused it. He suspected that eggs or spores may exist, which, lying dormant, would resist conditions that otherwise would kill the organisms. To prove this theory either right or wrong he made a pure culture of anthrax organisms in a sterilized blood-serum drop, placed it under the microscope, keeping it at the required temperature, and watched and waited. After twenty-four hours tiny threads appeared, developed into filaments and within the filaments rounded bodies appeared; these divided horizontally and each section contained one of these rounded bodies. Were they the spores he envisaged?

As a final test he dried the spores, put them aside for several weeks, and then placed them into a drop of ox-eye fluid and kept them at body temperature. Anthrax organisms as such could not have survived this treatment, but the spores slowly developed into the typical, thread-like shape of the anthrax bacillus, and proved as deadly as any taken from an animal that had just died of anthrax.

Koch's painstaking experiment had not only proved that anthrax is communicated by thread-like organisms, as had been already suspected, but also that they could lie dormant in the form of spores, to produce a new outbreak of the disease, perhaps after years.

He repeated his experiment again and again, to exclude any possible source of error and then, sure of his conclusions, wrote to Ferdinand Kohn, Professor of Botany at Breslau University, on April 22, 1876, asking if he may demonstrate to him some important findings. Kohn, who had already corresponded with Koch on various matters, agreed; with the result that, as Dr Koch's demonstrations progressed, he excitedly called in his colleague Kohnheim, Professor of Pathological Anatomy. Both these eminent scientists realised that a tremendous discovery had been made by Koch, and both were deeply impressed by the achievement of this young physician who had done an exacting piece of research entirely by himself and under the most primitive conditions.

The turning point had come. Dr Robert Koch was called to Breslau University; but he found that although conditions for research proved admirable, he could not make a living in Breslau. There followed a short return to Wollstein, after which he was invited to take up a post at the 'Kaiserliches Gesundheitsamt' (Imperial Department of Health) in Berlin, in 1880.

His career as a general practitioner was now at an end, that of a scientist and researcher of repute began. He initiated the use of micro-photography and of 'staining' (coloured slides), two entirely new methods of identifying and cataloguing bacteria; but his work was not entirely confined to the laboratory. He visited the famous Berlin Charité Hospital as a consultant, and in 1885 he became Director of the Institute of Infectious Diseases. He never lost his skill as a physician and colleagues at the Charité have described the meticulous, kindly way in which he examined each patient, supervised the treat-

147

ment and interested himself in the progress of each one.

In 1882, two years after his arrival in Berlin, Koch discovered the tuberculosis bacillus and made some other startling discoveries connected with this research; he found that the tuberculosis bacillus could thrive not only in lungs, but also in joints and intestines, and could even be present in patients who were not obviously suffering from any form of tuberculosis.

When he announced the results of his research to a meeting of the Physiological Society of Berlin, the most eminent scientists of Europe were present, and at the end of his deliberations the news travelled round the world, sent out by electric telegraph.

His invention of Tuberculin proved disappointing, though a modified version was later found to be of great value in the testing of cattle, and has made it possible to produce infection-free herds.

The discovery of the tuberculosis bacillus brought Robert Koch worldwide fame as a bacteriologist and when a cholera epidemic broke out in Egypt, his long suppressed desire to travel revived. Off he went to investigate the cause of the outbreak and to prevent the disease from spreading to Europe. He and his assistants eventually tracked down the origin of the epidemic and found it in India.

When they returned to Berlin in 1884 it was a triumph: they had discovered the 'comma' bacillus, which causes cholera, and had found its source in tainted water supplies. These discoveries did not produce a cure, but they did open up ways and means of preventing outbreaks of the disease.

The importance of Koch's work was recognised by the State and he received a reward of 100,000 marks – £5000 at the then current rate of exchange – a tidy sum of money in those days.

Egypt and India marked the beginning of many journeys. Emmy's continued protests were now in vain. Though in the early years their marriage had been happy enough, Robert was now no longer willing to give way to his wife and to curb his ardent wish to travel. The couple agreed to separate and Robert settled Emmy comfortably in Clausthal, her home town, which was exactly what she wanted.

In 1893 Robert married Hedwig Freiburg, a companion much more suited to his way of life by temperament and inclination than the all too stationary and unadventurous Emmy. Hedwig shared both Robert's scientific interests and his love of travel.

Africa was the next port of call, where malaria caused much sickness, especially among Europeans; then Koch was again sent to India, this time to trace the cause of bubonic plague. In East Africa he investigated a serious cattle plague, and similar outbreaks in the Transvaal, South Africa, and in Basutoland. He went to New Guinea, Java and the Carolinas, always in search of microbes, as well as to malaria ridden parts of Italy.

In 1900 he was back in Berlin to investigate an outbreak of typhus, only to be called to Africa again in 1903 as head of a research team sent out by the British Colonial Office; a venture which took two years to complete.

By now Dr Robert Koch was recognised as Europe's leading bacteriologist and in 1905 he received the Nobel Prize for his tuberculosis research. Shortly afterwards he was back in Africa as head of a Commission to investigate sleeping sickness.

Even at the age of sixty and over he still delighted in his life of travel and research. Slippers, armchair and retirement were not for him. In 1908 he decided on a trip round the world, but when he reached Japan he received a request from the German Minister of the Interior to attend a congress on tuberculosis in Washington, and to head the German delegation. This meant that he did not quite complete his journey round the globe; but he was received by the Mikado before he left Japan and had the pleasure of meeting again a former assistant he had much valued, the Japanese researcher Dr Kitasato.

His earth life was now drawing to a close. He was back

149

in Berlin in the autumn of 1908; but the strains and
stresses of his ever active life finally caught up with him
and he died of angina pectoris on the 27th of May 1910 in
the lovely Black Forest Spa of Baden-Baden, at the age of
sixty-six.

MARY

by Patricia Collins

A CHILD YOU'LL WANT
TO REMEMBER.

Mary Collins was a really beautiful baby. Born prematurely, she had a tiny oval face, a rosebud mouth and an enchanting smile. The third child of parents who came from the bustle of New York to make a home in Ireland, Mary found a warm and secure place in the heart of the family.

Then, eight months later, Patricia Collins learned that Mary was brain damaged. Doctors diagnosed cerebral palsy; she would probably never walk and she would almost certainly be retarded.

The shock of this discovery plunged Patricia into despair. Mary needed extensive therapy and the burden of caring for her increased Patricia's growing resentment and guilt — she began to drink heavily, blaming herself for what had happened. When circumstances forced the Collins family to return to America, Patricia made a wrenching decision to leave Mary behind in Ireland in a residential home for two years. The years in Ireland did nothing to lessen the severity of Mary's disabilities, but another kind of change did occur. Mary was becoming a determined, courageous child with a winning personality and she gave a very special purpose and meaning to life.

This is an intimate, inspiring and deeply moving account of a mother's journey from despair to joy and of the power of the human spirit to overcome adversity through love and understanding.

A STORY YOU WON'T FORGET.

BIOGRAPHY   0 7221 2482 1   **£1.50**

THE HEARTWARMING TRUE STORY
OF A VERY SPECIAL DOG
AND HER VERY SPECIAL OWNER

SHEILA HOCKEN

EMMA V.I.P.

(Illus)

Everyone knows the inspiring story of Sheila Hocken and her wonderful guide-dog Emma, and of the miracle operation which enabled her to see for the first time in her life.

Now, Sheila describes her life since the incredible moment when she opened her eyes and saw the beautiful world we all take for granted. With freshness and humour, Sheila tells how each day brought new joys, new challenges and new surprises.

Emma's life, too, has undergone dramatic changes. She was no longer needed as a guide-dog but her retirement has been far from idle. She is now a celebrity and receives her own fan mail; she has made several television appearances; she was Personality Dog of the Year at Crufts and is greeted in the street more often than Sheila is.

'Writing simply, with innate ability to externalise thought, feeling, experience, she again achieves a lovable intimacy'
Daily Telegraph

AUTOBIOGRAPHY   0 7221 4601 9   £1.25

Also by Sheila Hocken in Sphere Books:
EMMA AND I

A selection of bestsellers from SPHERE

FICTION

NIGHT PROBE!	Clive Cussler	£1.95 ☐
CHIMERA	Stephen Gallagher	£1.75 ☐
CALIFORNIA DREAMERS	Norman Bogner	£1.75 ☐
PALOMINO	Danielle Steel	£1.75 ☐
RAILROAD	Graham Masterton	£2.75 ☐

FILM & TV TIE-INS

SHARKY'S MACHINE	William Diehl	£1.75 ☐
WHOSE LIFE IS IT ANYWAY?	David Benedictus	£1.25 ☐
GREASE 2	William Rotsler	£1.25 ☐
CAT PEOPLE	Gary Brandner	£1.50 ☐

NON-FICTION

TOM PILGRIM: AUTOBIOGRAPHY OF A SPIRITUALIST HEALER	Tom Pilgrim	£1.50 ☐
YOUR CHILD AND THE ZODIAC	Teri King	£1.50 ☐
THE PAPAL VISIT	Timothy O'Sullivan	£2.50 ☐
THE SURVIVOR	Jack Eisner	£1.75 ☐

All Sphere books are available at your local bookshop or newsagent, or can be ordered direct from the publisher. Just tick the titles you want and fill in the form below.

Name _____

Address _____

_____

Write to Sphere Books, Cash Sales Department, P.O. Box 11, Falmouth, Cornwall TR10 9EN

Please enclose a cheque or postal order to the value of the cover price plus:

UK: 45p for the first book, 20p for the second book and 14p for each additional book ordered to a maximum charge of £1.63.

OVERSEAS: 75p for the first book plus 21p per copy for each additional book.

BFPO & EIRE: 45p for the first book, 20p for the second book plus 14p per copy for the next 7 books, thereafter 8p per book.

Sphere Books reserve the right to show new retail prices on covers which may differ from those previously advertised in the text or elsewhere, and to increase postal rates in accordance with the PO.